Building
Amsterdam

Written and illustrated by
Herman Janse

Translation by Sue Baker

Published by De Brink, Amsterdam

ISBN 90 216 7131 X

© Herman Janse Amsterdam, mcmxciv

Copyright of this edition: Uitgeverij
Ploegsma bv, mcmxciv
Translation: Sue Baker

Contents

The great city of Amsterdam is built on piles
and if the city falls, who will pay?
(Old Dutch poem)

The soil of Amsterdam

Around four hundred metres beneath Amsterdam lies a bed of hard rock which is millions of years old. Above this stretch thick layers of sand, deposited there during the Ice Age by glaciers from Scandinavia. When the ice retreated, tundra formed over which mammoths roamed until around 10,000 years ago. At the end of the Ice Age the sea level rose fifty metres in about 180,000 years, as the enormous amount of ice melted. The sea deposited layers of clay and sand containing shells. During the last 10,000 years marshes came into being in which peat was formed. Many trees lie in the peat, felled by the steady rise of the water. Through the centuries these have been well preserved and are still occasionally struck during pile driving for foundations.

The first sand layer beneath Amsterdam was formed during the last Ice Age and is around two and a half metres thick. This layer lies around twelve or thirteen metres beneath street level and can carry the weight of the foundations. Even today it is said during canal trips that the Oude Kerk (Old Church) was built at the end of the 13th century directly on a spur of the so-called Muider Sand, but this is not true. The walls were built on the thickly packed peat.

The upper subsoil in the centre of Amsterdam was formed by embankments created by the earliest inhabitants and the waste they left behind. Sometimes these are interrupted by thin layers of clay from flooding.

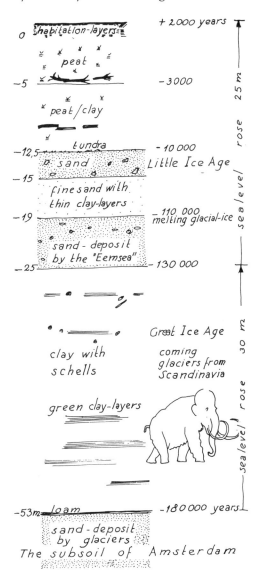

The subsoil of Amsterdam

Origins of the city

In the 12th century the low lying marshland was regularly ravaged by storm tides. The level of the water rose steadily and the lakes gradually ate further into the soft land. Tidal inlets were formed and the Flevomeer (Flevo lake) grew into a completely new inner sea, the Zuiderzee.

An arm of sea between the Zuiderzee and the coastal dunes split the former county of Holland in two. The waters of the coastal area had short names like Aa, Ee or Ye. Place names such as Ter Aar, Edam and Krommenie

(crooked Ye) still bear witness to this. The arm of sea was also known as the Ye, which later changed into Y or IJ. Through the area of peat and clay between the original course of the river Rhine at Woerden and the IJ meandered a river called the Aa or Ame. At the end of the 12th century people began to inhabit and cultivate the stretch of marshland south of the IJ, which was given the name Amestelle, area on the Ame. There was also a village called Tamen, now a part of Uithoorn. The east bank of the river was called Ouder-Amstel (Old Amstel); the west bank Nieuwer-Amstel (New Amstel). Gradually the river also came to be known as the Amstel. In the 12th

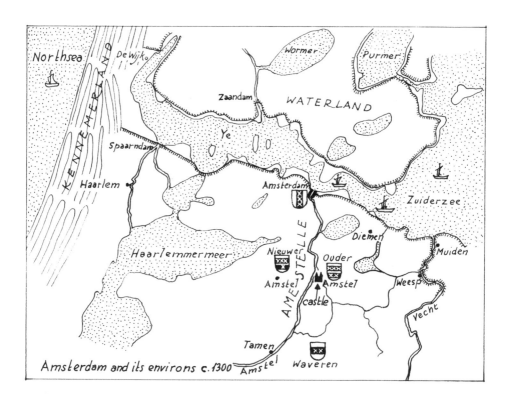

Amsterdam and its environs c.1300

century a church was built near the castle of the rulers of this area (the Lords of Amstel). In the 13th century a castle was built near the IJ and at the end of the century a second church was built in Amestelle. The village around the first church was given the name Ouderkerk (Old Church).

The region often flooded and the water posed a growing threat to the marshlands of Holland. A solution had to be found for the unlimited flow of water from higher ground and for the threat from the sea. Accordingly dams and dikes (the Dutch word is dijk) were raised, for instance along the IJ and the Amstel. Street names like Haarlemmerdijk, Nieuwendijk and Zeedijk show where these dikes ran. It is even possible to see where they were: the alleyways between the Nieuwezijds Voorburgwal and the Nieuwendijk slope upwards.

A dam was built in the Amstel to prevent high tides flooding the land, and the neighbouring town was called Amestelledamme. It was inhabited mainly by fishermen, artisans and traders. The straight stretch (rak) of the river outside the dam was called Damrak; the stretch inside the dam was Rak-in, now Rokin.

The excess water around Nieuwer-Amstel flowed along a peat channel, the Boerenwetering, in the direction of Amsterdam and to the IJ. To hold back the sea water and to allow water from the land to drain into the open sea, a lock was built in the dam. During its construction, the river water had to be temporarily drained along another route. It is probable that a link was dug

between the Amstel and the Boeren-wetering, which has become known as Spui. A detour was also dug on the other side. Together they created an ideal border for the growing settlement around the Dam in the Amstel.

In 1274 the inhabitants were granted freedom from tolls in all Holland by Count Floris V. In 1306 the village was given town rights.

The first church in Amsterdam was built on land behind the dike east of the Amstel and was dedicated to Saint Nicholas, patron saint of seafarers and traders. He is also the patron saint of the city. Later another church was built on the west bank of the Amstel. The first house of prayer is still known as the Oude Kerk (Old Church) and the second as the Nieuwe Kerk (New Church).

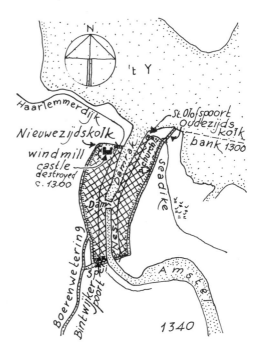

Growth of the city

The young Amsterdam was protected on both sides of the Amstel by earthen walls (burgwal) along the canals. Their names were taken from the side of the canal on which they lay: Oudezijds (old side) and Nieuwezijds (new side) Burgwal. The city was enlarged around 1380 and a second walled canal was created on the Oude Zijde, the Oudezijds Achterburgwal. When the first defensive wall fell out of use, the Oude Kerk could be extended eastwards, although there was not quite enough space. The canal wall was curved around the choir of the church. You can still see the bend in the canal wall.

More extra ground was added on the Nieuwe Zijde, stretching to the Nieuwezijds Achterburgwal.

By 1420 the city was again too small.

A new wall was built on the eastern side along what is now the Geldersekade and the Kloveniersburgwal. A moat (singel) was excavated on the western side which Amsterdammers have insisted on calling the Singel.

In 1578 Amsterdam embraced the new reformed religion, one of the last cities in the west of the Netherlands to do so. Despite the continuing war against Catholic Spain, the city flourished. From the IJ, countless ships set forth to sail the world. The goods they brought back were stored and traded in the Amstel city. There was, however, one big problem: not enough space within the old walls.

Outside the ramparts on the eastern side was a stretch of land used for shipbuilding, rope-making (on rope walks or lijnbanen) and drying dyed materials. This area, known as the Lastage (Burden) from the loading of ships, was brought within the city in 1585. Excavation of a canal outside the Singel (the Herengracht) was begun the same year. This area was also given a

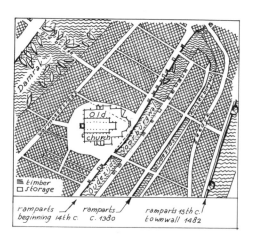

ramparts beginning 14th c.   ramparts c. 1380   ramparts 15th c. town wall 1482

line of defensive earthworks. In 1593 a new area on the eastern side was brought within the city walls. Canals were dug and space created for warehouses and factories.

Amsterdam had 30,000 inhabitants in 1580. In just 50 years the figure rose to 125,000. In 1612, with expansion taking place on the west side of the city where two new canals (the Keizersgracht and the Prinsengracht) were being dug, the city was flooded with refugees from the Southern Netherlands eager to escape the laws of the Spanish rulers and the Roman Catholic Church. Small canals and streets were hastily constructed among the existing ditches of the polderland outside the city, where the refugees could build their simple houses. These streets and canals were mostly named after a flower or a plant. When French refugees arrived in 1685 and also settled in this area, they called it Jardin, because the street names made them feel as if they were in a garden. The name was later distorted into Jordaan.

The expansion of 1612, when the city doubled its size, was brought to a temporary halt with the creation of a side canal, the Leidsegracht.

A major expansion took place around 1660, when canals to the south and east of the centre were dug. This was finished off with the Lijnbaansgracht and bordered by a new wall and outer canal. In this way, and as if naturally, the semi-circle of canals and the concentric streets grew up around the mediaeval centre; a layout for which Amsterdam has been famous for centuries and which served Peter the Great as a model when he created St. Petersburg.

In the 17th century, to the east and west, islands were created in the IJ for warehouses and factories: another way of extending the boundaries of the city. This created more than enough space and no further expansion was necessary until the middle of the 19th century. From 1850 the Amsterdam population suddenly increased so rapidly that new housing areas were needed outside the outer canal. A major expansion was begun in 1920, with new districts named after the points of the compass: Amsterdam West, South and East. New districts were also established north of the IJ. The city has grown so explosively since the Second World War that a new town even had to be built in the polders south of the city: the Bijlmermeer.

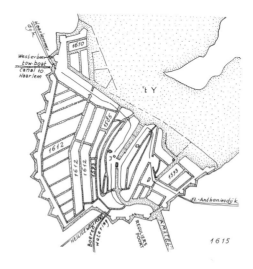

City walls and gates

The oldest town had three gates (a gate is a poort in Dutch). The Sint-Olofs-poort, named after the adjoining chapel of the Norwegian sailors, stood where the eastern Amsteldijk becomes the Zeedijk. The second gate, the Haarlemmerpoort, was on the spot where the western Amsteldijk, the Nieuwendijk (new dike), becomes the IJdijk, which at this point is called the Haarlemmerdijk. At the Spui stood the Bintwijkerpoort, which gave access to the Binnenwijk (inner quarter).
After the development in the 14th and 15th centuries the city was still protected by earthen walls and rows of wooden palisades. In the 15th century

gunpowder was invented, but it was not until 1480, when the fleets of Amsterdam and Gelderland joined battle on the Zuiderzee and the Bishop of Utrecht's troops threatened the city, that the authorities decided to build brick walls. The section between the IJ and the sea-dike was given the name Gelderse (from Gelderland) kade and one of the towers along the wall was called 'Silent Utrecht'.
The cost of Amsterdam's brick wall was raised by fines in the form of money or bricks. The wall was vaulted on the inner side. On top ran a wallwalk with a parapet as protection against enemy bullets. You can still see loopholes for rifles and cannon in the remaining buildings of the wall.
Towers giving a clear view of the area immediately in front of the wall stood

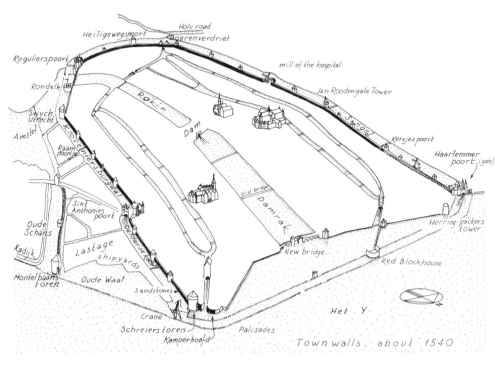

Town walls. about 1540

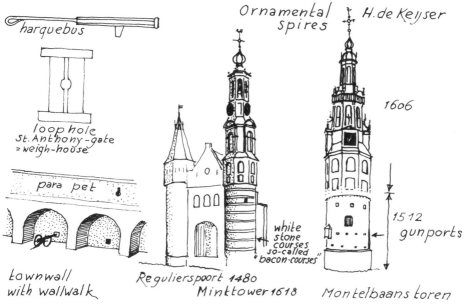

harquebus

loophole
St. Anthony-gate
= weigh-house

para pet

townwall
with wallwalk

Ornamental spires — H. de Keyser

Regulierspoort 1480
Minttower 1618

white
stone
courses
so-called
"bacon-courses"

1606

1512 gunports

Montelbaans toren

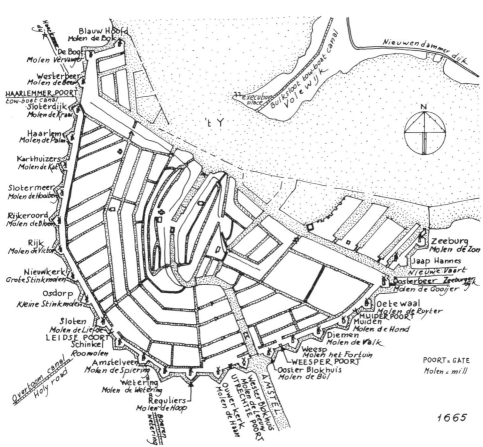

Blauw Hoofd
Molen de Bok

De Boot
Molen Vervang...

Westerbeer
Molen de Beer

HAARLEMMER POORT
tow-boat canal
Sloterdijk
Molen de Kraai

Haarlem
Molen de Palm

Karthuizers
Molen de Kat

Slotermeer
Molen de Hooiberg

Rijkeroord
Molen de Bloem

Rijk
Molen de Victor

Nieuwkerk
Grote Stinkmolen

Osdorp
Kleine Stinkmolen

Sloten
Molen de Liefde
LEIDSE POORT
Schinkel
Roomolen

Amstelveen
Molen de Spiering

Wetering
Molen de Wetering

Reguliers
Molen de Hoop

Overtoom canal
Holy road

Nieuwendammer dijk

execution
place

Buiksloot tow-boat canal
Volewijk

'tY

N

Zeeburg
Molen de Zon

Jaap Hannes
Nieuwe Vaart

Oosterbeer Zeeburg...
Molen de Goojjer

Oetewaal
Molen de Ruyter

MUIDER POORT
Muiden
Molen de Hond

Diemen
Molen de Valk

Weesp
Molen het Fortuin
WEESPER POORT

Ooster Blokhuis
Molen de Bijl

Wester Blokhuis
Molen de Leeuw
UTRECHTSE POORT
Ouwer-kerk
Molen de Haan

AMSTEL

Booren
Wetering

POORT = GATE
Molen = mill

1665

11

at regular intervals. There was a gate at irregular intervals. The entrance of the sea-dike was protected to the east by the Sint-Anthoniespoort, and to the west by a new Haarlemmerpoort. Under each gate was a sluice for draining excess water into the IJ.

On the Singel at the Amstel stood the Regulierspoort, a rectangular building flanked by two towers. The gate was named after the monastry of the Reguliers, which stood just outside the city. After a fire in 1619, virtually the whole building was demolished. All that remained was the tower nearest to the Amstel. City architect Hendrick de Keijser designed an ornamental spire and a sentry box was added. In the crisis year of 1672, when the city was threatened by the French, the sentry box was used for minting coins. This continued for less than two years but the building and tower are still known as the Munt (the Mint).

The corner tower on the IJ acquired the name Schreierstoren. This name is said to come from the weeping (schreiende) women who waved farewell to their seafaring menfolk from this spot. In fact the tower stands where two canals meet to form a sharp bend: a 'schrey-hoeck' in old Dutch. In modern Dutch the word 'schrey' can be found in 'schrijlings' which means straddling. Unwelcome ships were kept outside city waters by a double row of palisades in the IJ. But the only protection afforded the Lastage between the sea-dike and the IJ was an earthen wall, despite the area's importance to Amsterdam's well-being, with its work-places and trades. In 1512, after yet another attack by the Gelderlanders, realization dawned that the existing protection was inadequate. A free-standing tower was built in which protective artillary was placed. Not long afterwards, and shortly before the city gained its freedom from the Spanish yoke in 1578, the rulers themselves devised a plan to build a castle in the Lastage to keep the Amsterdammers under control. Monte Albano (white mountain) was to be its name. This name was later given to the defensive tower and has been distorted into Montelbaanstoren.

The old city wall was enclosed by the new walls after 1600 and lost its original function. With the exception of a few sections, the old wall was demolished. What remained was given a new use. Some of the remaining towers were given ornamental spires. The Sint-Anthoniespoort was refashioned as the Waag (weigh-house) and the square in front of it became a market, the Nieuwmarkt (New Market). The space between the front gate and the main gate was roofed over. A cupola was built over the main gate in 1692, under which the guild of surgeons held its meetings. The guild of masons also had a guild room there, which still exists.

And still Amsterdam was not sufficiently protected. Weapons had become so powerful in the 17th century that a brick wall did not offer enough resistance. As a reinforcement, a new girdle was constructed on the furthest outer rim of the city along the outer canal. It had earthen walls with 26 bastions, each with a windmill. Five new gates were built. The foundations of the Muiderpoort suddenly collapsed in 1769. The replacement gate is now the only one of the five still standing. In the 19th century the whole city wall was removed. Some sections were turned into gardens. The Haarlemmerpoort was replaced in 1840 with the Willemspoort, a triumphal gate marking the coronation of King Willem II.

The city gates had lost their defensive function; they served mainly as a source of tax. When the municipal tax was abolished in 1866, the gates lost their final function.

Haarlemmerpoort
1481-1612

Regulierspoort
1481-1619

St.-Anthoniespoort
1481   (Waag)

Haarlemmerpoort
H. de Keyser 1615-1837

Leidsepoort
D. Stalpaert 1661-1862

Utrechtse   poort
Weesper   G.Bz Swanenburg
(Muider   1660-1859
†1769

Willemspoort
C. Alewijn 1840

poort = gate
Town-gates

Muiderpoort
C. Rauws 1770

Building styles and architects

The earliest predominant building style in Amsterdam was characterized by pointed arches and vertical features, later known as Gothic. Buildings from this period not only have vertical lines but also distinct horizontal sections. They have a plinth, a water sill under the windows and a horizontal cornice to finish off each storey. The only example of fully developed Gothic, as found particularly in France and Germany, is the Nieuwe Kerk on the Dam. The central sections of this cruciform basilica with their wooden vaults soar high above the lower wings of stone vaulting. Although the church was given a 17th century facelift after the fire of 1645, it still retained its predominantly late-mediaeval character. The Oude Kerk was a much more local design, best seen in the vaulted wooden ceilings, the so-called barrel vaults. The building was extended repeatedly between 1300 and 1560; the result is a less than harmonious yet picturesque example of the regional style, which could be called Polder-Gothic.

The first signs of Renaissance, a style taken from Roman architecture, appeared around 1535 in Amsterdam. The north top gable of the Nieuwe Kerk, built around 1540, illustrates how slowly a building style develops. The large window still has a Gothic form with Gothic-like divisions, but pillars, triangular pediments, shell motifs and candelabra are placed more or less arbitrarily in some sections of the façade and the corner buttresses. The typical Dutch Renaissance developed in this way between 1535 and 1640. Features from classical architecture were amalgamated into a more or less picturesque style, which shows in the contrast between yellow sandstone and orange-red brick. The characteristic horizontal lines are, however, still broken up by mediaeval-looking vertical accents and rounded semi-circular and basket-handle arches. An unmistakable example is the new crown which Joost Jansz Bilhamer designed in 1565 for the tower of the Oude Kerk. The many small pediments and the monumental dials cannot detract from its vertical character.

A typical feature is the so-called strap-work, which played a prominent role in the architecture of this period. It can be seen in the work of Hendrick de Keijser, the most important architect of the time. He was city mason and sculptor from 1595. In fact he was city architect and designed many churches, public buildings and houses.

Flourishing trade and the many new inhabitants led to an enormous amount of building work. The interiors of old Catholic churches were adapted to the new reformed religion and the city expansions included new churches for the fast growing population. One of these was erected in 1668 as a temporary wooden church: the Amstel-kerk on the Amstelveld. But just as with other temporary buildings, it is still there.

Architects like Jacob van Campen arrived back in Amsterdam around 1630 from study tours of Italy and

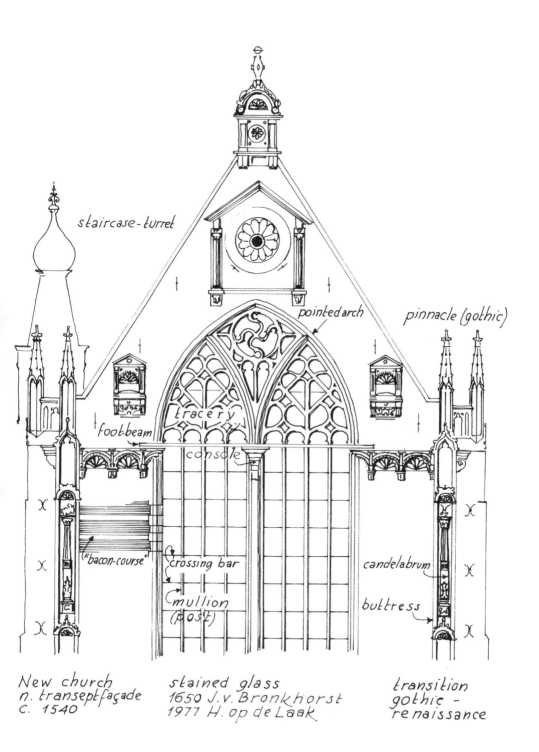

staircase-turret

pointed arch

pinnacle (gothic)

tracery

foot-beam

console

"bacon-course"

crossing bar

candelabrum

mullion (post)

buttress

New church
n. transeptfaçade
c. 1540

stained glass
1650 J.v.Bronkhorst
1977 H. op de Laak

transition
gothic -
renaissance

began developing a much more austere style: Dutch Classicism. Its ideal was a symmetric design with simple proportions. They added to this classical pilasters (square, flat pillars which protrude slightly from the wall), which sometimes ran through more than one storey. The Palace on the Dam is one of the most important examples of this style, but it can also be found in the façades of houses, among others those of the architects Philips and Justus Vingboons.

Classic columns on a building should follow a strict pattern, starting at the bottom and working upwards: Doric, Ionic, Corinthian, Composite. But this rule was often broken. Jacob van Campen for example gave the first two storeys above the ground floor of the Palace a colossal order of Composite pilasters with above them Corinthian. Because Dutch Classicism used features from Roman architecture, a remarkable conflict arose. The Romans used a roof gradient of about 22 degrees, with a triangular closure: a pediment. In the rainy Dutch climate, a pitch of 50 to 60 degrees was needed. Even so, Dutch architects made use of the pediment, but only as an ornament. In this way a wide classical building was given a pediment on its front façade, above which rose the actual roof. When zinc became more affordable in the 19th century a lower pitch was possible and buildings could be constructed with the 'Roman' pitched roof.

From 1665 onwards, Adriaan Dortsman designed the first large buildings and wide houses without pilasters and horizontal cornices. This architecture was totally defined by the rhythmic arrangement of the windows. The walls of the façade are still closed off at the top with a horizontal cornice in the classical style.

Dortsman ushered in a new period. Since that time house façades have been ornamented with features from the prevailing style of the era in which they were built. On the earliest façades late-Classicism is still in evidence, but from the end of the 17th century the influence of the French kings became apparent. Louis XIV's style can be recognized from symmetric scrolls.

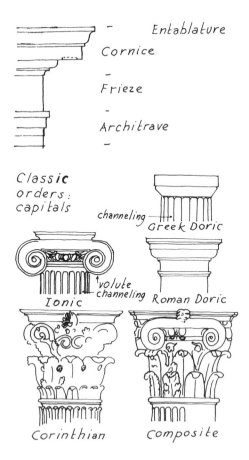

Entablature
Cornice
Frieze
Architrave

Classic orders: capitals

channeling — Greek Doric
volute channeling — Roman Doric
Ionic
Corinthian
Composite

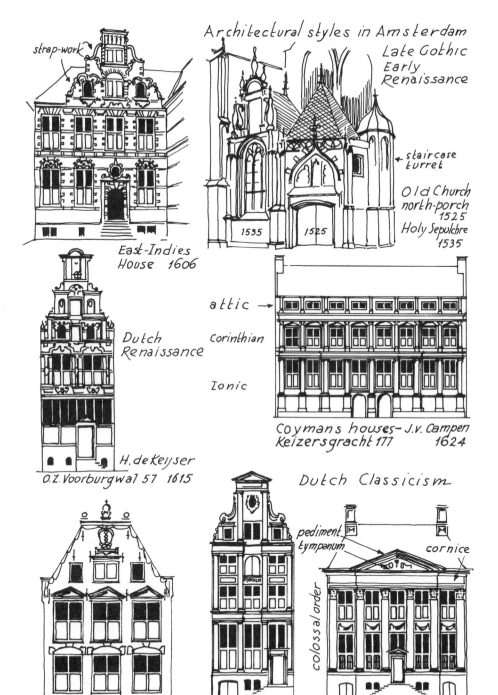

strap-work

East-Indies House 1606

Architectural styles in Amsterdam
Late Gothic
Early Renaissance

staircase turret

Old Church north-porch 1525
Holy Sepulchre 1535

1535   1525

Dutch Renaissance

attic →

Corinthian

Ionic

Coymans houses – J.v. Campen
Keizersgracht 177   1624

H. de Keyser
O.Z. Voorburgwal 57 1615

Dutch Classicism

pediment
tympanum

cornice

colossal order

Serge-hall Staalstraat
1641 Pieter de Keyser

Oude Turfmarkt
1642 Philip Vingboons
original designs

Kloveniersburgwal 95
1642

17

simplified Classicism
A. Dortsman

Louis-XIV
symmetric
heavy lines
1700

Régence
motives
1725

Louis-XV
asymmetric
fine lines
1750 1775

Damrak 83
Louis-XVI — Classicism
Felix Meritis-J.O.Husly 1778

C. Outshoorn 1860 Keizergracht 452
Eclecticism

Neo-Gothic

ca. 1880
I. Gosschalk
Reguliersgracht 57

Damrak 62 1886
Neo-Renaissance

J. F. Staal 1915
Herengr. 545-549

Amsterdam School

H. Ronnerplein 1920

18

Around 1725 the space between edges and scrolls was filled with diamond or scale motifs in the style of the regency which ruled after Louis XIV and before Louis XV. This is known as Regency.
A more graceful style arrived from France around 1750. The scrolls were now more delicate and the crests asymmetrical, as if the wind had blown them awry. This style is known as Louis XV. A shell motif was often used for which the French name was rocaille and this style became known as Rococo.
After extravagance came sobriety. A stateliness appeared in architecture around 1775, again with classical forms. This new development was first apparent in the Louis XVI style with its disciplined garlands and severe classical cornices.
Few buildings in the Empire style inspired by Napoleon were constructed in the Netherlands, because prosperity had declined drastically during French rule.
The first half of the 19th century was mainly dominated by neo-classicism. In the latter half of that century many architects reached back to earlier styles, although they did not all use features from the same style. This led to the neo-styles: neo-Gothic, neo-Renaissance and neo-Classicism. The combination of historic ornaments and new ideas created a new style: Eclecticism. The famous architects of the time were Pierre J.H. Cuypers and A.L. van Gendt, who designed typical neo-buildings like the Rijksmuseum, Central Station and the Concertgebouw. Hendrik Petrus Berlage made his debut with eclectic designs, but broke new ground around 1900 with the Beurs (Exchange), a model of honest and visible use of building materials such as brick, natural stone and steel. His buildings ushered in contemporary architecture. Moreover, brick began to play an important role, at first in the Amsterdam School (1910-1940). Architects like Michel de Klerk and Piet Kramer moulded, as it were, in brick, wood and iron. They used everything in the service of the form, with the result that the construction itself was often bad. It was discovered later just how deficient the water resistance of the brickwork was. They paid much attention to working class housing. Amsterdam Council had many schools and bridges built in this style.
With the arrival of reinforced concrete and steel, a style of architecture developed from 1920 which took as its starting point functional use of materials, constructions and spaces. This severe design is mainly known as New Building or New Realism.

The Dam

Back in 1380 there was no large square in the centre of Amsterdam, as there is now. But expansion of the city at that time created space on the site where the oldest city wall had stood. Willem Eggert – banker, counsellor and financier to Count Willem VI of Holland – offered his garden between the Nieuwendijk and the Nieuwezijds Voorburgwal for the building of a new church. This Gothic building, completed around 1450 and dedicated to the Holy Catharina, is still called the Nieuwe Kerk (New Church). The church has been extended several times but was never given a tower. South of the church lay a churchyard, used for burials until the 16th century.

The original dam in the Amstel was totally rebuilt around 1540, although the sea still had free access up to the dam. Traders and fishermen could unload their goods from small ships for sale in the city centre or on the fish market on the covered Damsluis (Dam lock).

West of the dam was a small square called the Place, where the city hall stood with its open hall of columns and a tower. The growth of the city also created space problems for its government and the hospital behind the city hall was bought to enable expansion to take place.

More space came free on the small square in 1565 when a number of houses between Damrak and Nieuwendijk were demolished. A weigh-house was constructed on this land where goods could be weighed. In contrast to the Gothic Nieuwe Kerk and city hall, the weigh-house was Dutch Renaissance.

An exchange was built over the water of the Rokin in 1609, designed by Hendrick de Keijser. Goods were traded and other business transacted in the courtyard and under the galleries.

The Nieuwe Kerk was burned down in 1645 through the carelessness of a plumber who was soldering a lead gutter on the roof. Rebuilding was soon begun and completed three years later. There were plans to give the church a tower, but they got no further than four heavy pillars. Two of these were demolished in 1783. The lack of remaining space on the Voorburgwal was solved by building a very wide bridge over it: the Donkere Sluis (Dark bridge).

Once the Nieuwe Kerk was completed, work began behind the old city hall on a large new building for the city government. It was designed by Jacob van Campen in a severe classical style. When the old city hall burned down a few years later, work was speeded up to get the new building finished. It was opened for use in 1655. All the surrounding buildings were demolished, bringing the Nieuwe Kerk directly on to the Dam. These two buildings created a fantastic increase in scale in the heart of the city. The weigh-house lost its balustrade and was given a new roof in 1776, but otherwise no radical changes took place around the Dam until 1808.

In that year Louis Napoleon became

King of Holland. He wanted a palace in the capital city. The city had no money for a new building and offered, on a temporary basis, the city hall. The weigh-house was demolished to give the King a better view. Right up to the present day the Dutch royal family continues to use the former city hall as a Royal Palace, with inaugurations taking place in the Nieuwe Kerk. Down the years the city government had to be content with offices in the Prinsenhof between the Oudezijds Voorburgwal and Achterburgwal, formerly the seat of the Admirality. It was not until 1987 that a new city hall was built on the Amstel. It is combined with a music theatre and is known to the locals as the Stopera.

The foundations of the Exchange, built in the waters of the Amstel, began to subside severely and in 1838 the

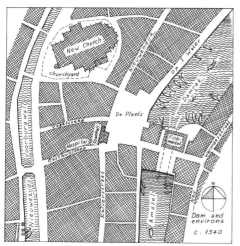

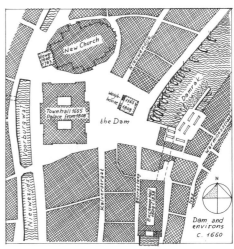

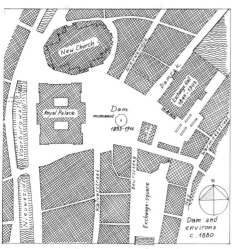

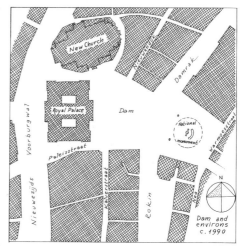

building had to be demolished. A piece of the Damrak near the Dam was filled in, as a result of which the water no longer reached the Dam. A new Exchange was built on this land, designed by the garden architect from Haarlem, Johann David Zocher.

The battle of 1830 against the Belgians was commemorated in 1853 with an ugly Unity monument which was soon christened 'Naatje' by the Amster-dammers. The designer was H.M. Tetar van Elven, whose father designed the six monumental cast iron lampposts which still stand around the Palace. Great changes took place between 1900 and 1914. Another piece of the Damrak had already been filled in and work now started on the building of a new Exchange, this one designed by Berlage. When the building was opened in 1903, the old Exchange was demolished.

Around 1912 virtually all the old

Dam about 1600

Dam about 1780

buildings around the square were demolished. The Unity monument, by now missing one arm and known locally as 'Naatje one arm', made way for the 'electric tram'. And the buildings of the covered Damsluis were demolished to make the Dam into a large square. The National Monument was built after the Second World War in memory of the victims. In this way the Dam developed into the National Square of the Netherlands.

Exchange Hall by Hendrick de Keyser

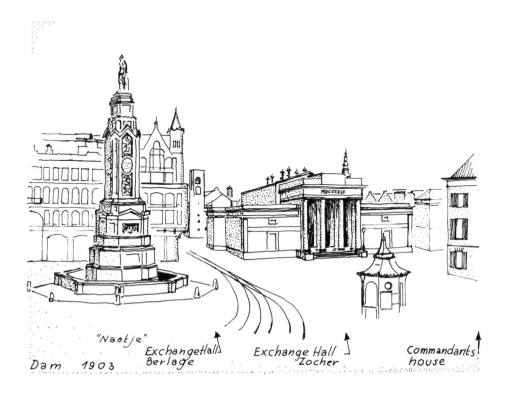

Dam 1903   "Naatje"   Exchangehall Berlage   Exchange Hall Zocher   Commandants house

The fire service

The first houses were built from wood and had thatched roofs of reeds or straw. A distinct fire hazard, if only because the fire for cooking and heating was situated in the middle of the floor of the house. One spark was enough to reduce a complete neighbourhood into ash. After two major fires in the 15th century, the city fathers issued strict regulations. From then on the houses had to have brick side walls and roofs had to be covered with non-flammable materials. Subsidies were even available for this. Where the roof was still thatched, it had to be covered with clay. One regulation dated 1521 stipulated that all remaining wooden houses should be replaced with brick buildings. Only wooden gables were still allowed.

The Oude Kerk (Old Church) has never been damaged by fire. As a result, the unique roof dating from the 14th to the 16th centuries has remained intact. Inside the church is the so-called Iron Chapel, a fireproof storage area for the city archives. Documents from these archives show that from the mid-16th century there had to be a gap of at least 70 cm between two houses, to allow space for water to drip from the eaves. Rain water from the roofs could run into this space and drain away. Side walls had to be no thinner than one Gouda brick of 18 cm.

For a long time fire fighting remained a primitive affair. Leather buckets stood at designated places in every neighbourhood and were used to scoop water from the canals. Chains of people were formed to pass the buckets from hand to hand to the fire. Special hooks were used to pull down burning parts of buildings.

It was only in 1672, when the Amsterdam painter Jan van der Heyden invented the linen hose with which water could be sprayed directly onto the fire, that fire fighting became easier. His invention was later perfected by the addition of the vacuum pump. Fire buckets remained available, however, in every block of houses until the end of the 18th century. It took until 1870 before the city had four horse-drawn steam-driven fire engines.

As far as possible, storage space for flammable materials had to be built on the outskirts of the city. For example, tar warehouses on Prinsen Island. Yet many warehouses still burned down. Amsterdam's most beautiful warehouse, the Korendrager (corn holder) on the Oude Schans, was filled with corks when it burned down in 1949. Important buildings were regularly lost to fire. In the mid-17th century two burned down shortly after each other: the Nieuwe Kerk through the carelessness of a plumber and, seven years later, the old city hall on the Dam. In 1772 fire destroyed the theatre on the Keizersgracht and in 1890 the new, wooden theatre on the Leidseplein burned down. The 17th century marine magazine went up in flames in 1791 but was immediately rebuilt and now houses the Maritime Museum. The round Lutheran Church burned down in 1822. When it was rebuilt, it was again adorned with its distinctive copper-plated cupola.

A number of important buildings have also been lost to fire in the 20th century. The Paleis voor Volksvlijt (Palace of Public Events), built between 1859 and 1864 and modelled on the Crystal Palace in London, went up in flames in the bitter winter of 1929. Constructed mainly out of cast iron and glass, it stood on the spot where once the Utrecht gate had stood. The Netherlands Bank now stands there. The Berlage-designed building of C&A on the Damrak burned down in the winter of 1963 and the late-mediaeval Sint-Olofskapel, one of the oldest buildings in the city, in 1966. This last fire was the result of welding supports needed to keep the building from collapsing! The chapel was rebuilt in 1992.

New Church after fire 1645

Fire-engine of Jan van der Heyden

Leather fire-bucket

Locks

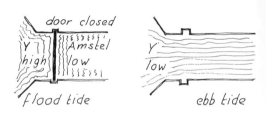

door closed

Y high | Amstel low

flood tide

Y low

ebb tide

The first locks were very simple. They consisted of a square opening in the dam with a wooden sliding gate. At low water, the gate slid upwards to allow surplus water to drain away. These locks are known as a sluice. The speed with which the water drained away prevented the harbour from silting up. The gates of these sluices hung on strong ropes from an axle. This could be turned by hand with a spoke, although big gates were hard work. To make raising easier, a large wheel was sometimes fixed to each end of the spoke in which a man could walk. If he walked forwards, the wheel under his feet turned and the hoisting rope wound around the axle.

There were sluices like this at the Dam, the Sint-Anthoniespoort and the Haarlemmerpoort. The Oudezijds and the Nieuwezijds Burgwallen also drained their water into the IJ in this way.

Lock gates were later made to swing on a vertical axle, just like ordinary gates. Large locks have two gates which fit together at their outer edges. A long pole on the winch sets them in motion so that they can be closed at high tide. There are even locks where the gates close to the pressure of rising tide or inland water. They are called ebb and flood gates.

There are also lift-locks with room between the gates for a ship. This space is called the lock-chamber. These locks are designed to adjust the height of the

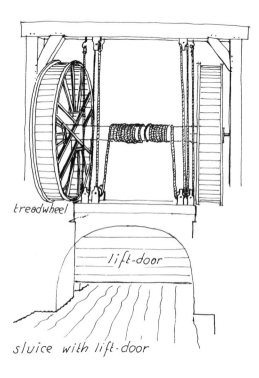

treadwheel

lift-door

sluice with lift-door

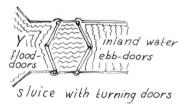

Y flood-doors

inland water ebb-doors

sluice with turning doors

26

water so that the ship can sail on. With the gates at both ends closed, the water in the lock-chamber is brought to the level of that on which the ship floats. The gates open at that end and the ship sails into the lock. When all the gates are shut, the water and the ship are taken up or down to the level at the other end.

It is likely that lift-locks along the direct link between the Amsterdam polder and the IJ were not built until the 16th century. Lift-locks were built in the Amstel in the late-17th century as part of large-scale water regulations in Amsterdam. The water in the Amsterdam canals was not very clean, because waste water from houses drained into them. The network of locks was – and still is – used to flush the canals daily. Because water from the IJ was used to flush the Amsterdam canals, these were often salty. Water for washing floors, steps and windows was usually taken from the canals, which did little for the long term quality of the brick walls and glass windows because of salt damage. Drinking water was delivered by barge.

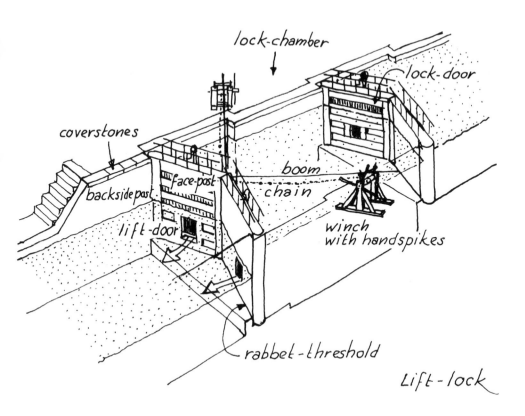

Lift-lock

Bridges

In a city with a river and many canals, bridges provide an essential link between the countless islands. The earliest bridges were for pedestrians only. Goods traffic in the form of hand-carts and horse-drawn wagons and sledges came later. There is a woodcut map of Amsterdam dated 1544 on which 35 bridges can be counted. Now there are 1300, of which 113 have names.

The oldest bridges were timber beam bridges. A number of trusses, consisting of two slanting posts with a beam laid across them, were driven into the water. Other beams were laid from truss to truss, and planks to form the roadway were nailed on top. The section between the last truss and the quay was often extended to one side for use as a boathouse or storage area.

In the trading city of Amsterdam goods were carried by water. Ships had to be able to pass under the bridges, in many cases with their sails hoisted as lowering them cost too much time. This was the case, for example, along the Damrak, the Kloveniersburgwal at the Silent Utrecht tower and at the Schreierstoren. An opening was made in the middle of the bridge and filled with a section which could be raised or lowered. This was known as a 'bridge gap'. A bridge gap was not strong enough to bear the weight of a wagon. As early as the beginning of the 16th century leaf bridges were being built along various traffic routes. Where

wide ships had to pass under a bridge, double leaf bridges with two movable sections were built. The Magere Bridge (literally thin but meaning narrow in this case) over the Amstel is an example of a double leaf bridge.

A fixed bridge in front of the city gates would have given easy access to the canals to any enemies. For this reason a movable section was made to span the distance between the fixed part of the bridge and the gate.

Wooden bridges were often named for the colour in which they were painted. The bridge over the Amstel near the modern city hall/music theatre was blue, and the richly ornamented 19th century replacement stone bridge is still called the Blue Bridge.

Wood that protrudes above water rots away and bridges often needed repairing. A great step forward was made when bridges were built from brick and stone. The foundations were constructed by damming an area in the water. The water was pumped out and the pile driving carried out. Once this was done, the first bricks were laid beneath water level. Once the water was freed around the pillars, the rest of the brickwork was completed. Arches of sandstone and brick were made between the pillars. Sand was then thrown down and the pavement laid. In Amsterdam these tall stone bridges are called a 'sluis', which has nothing to do with a sluice or lift-lock. There is the Torensluis where a tower (the Jan Rodenpoortstoren) once stood, and the Hoge (Tall) Sluis where the city wall meets the Amstel.

The Hoge Sluis was replaced around

1860 with a richly ornamented bridge of iron beams and two movable sections. Many other bridges were replaced by lower iron beam bridges because motorized traffic, particularly trams, could not negotiate the steep 'cat backs'. But the steep bridges along the Amstel and the Reguliersgracht still give a flavour of olden days. Amsterdam's widest bridge is now the Muntplein. In front of the Reguliers-poort lay a wooden leaf bridge, which was replaced in 1635 with a stone arched bridge. This remained in use until the horse-drawn tram arrived in 1876 and proved unable to climb the steep bridge. The bridge was replaced with a wider and lower iron beam bridge. Since then it has been drastically widened several times to its present 70 metres.

In the 19th century beautiful bridges were constructed from cast iron, some of which are still standing. Leaf bridges, too, were made from iron. When one of these needed widening in 1955, it was given a relatively light platform of aluminium.

In the Amsterdam School period before 1940, many bridges were richly ornamented with wonderful brick-work, sculpture and skillfully wrought railings. They have their own special place in the cityscape.

Nowadays the bridges that open over the Amsterdam shipping routes are often variations on the counter-poise bridge: the counterweight of the movable section fits into a cellar under the street surface. There are also some lift bridges where the whole of the bridge surface is lifted up between four towers.

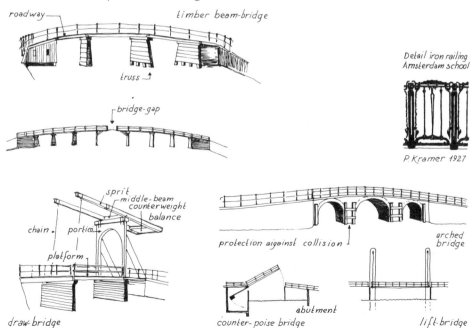

roadway — timber beam-bridge

truss →

bridge-gap

Detail iron railing Amsterdam school

P. Kramer 1927

sprit
middle-beam
counterweight
balance
chain — portico
platform

protection against collision →

arched bridge

abutment

draw-bridge

counter-poise bridge

lift-bridge

The Open IJ and land reclamation

The original IJ was a channel in a landscape of mudflats between Flevo-meer and Zandvoort, in which ebb and flood tides flowed freely. Sometime around the year 1000 the North Sea coast opening silted up and the line of dunes closed. The IJ then formed a bay in the Zuiderzee. It remained open sea, governed by tides. The Damrak in Amsterdam was also tidal and the water of the Geldersekade and in the ditches of the Lastage was open to the sea. This area of the city was then very much like the Venice of today.

Virtually the whole city was closed off from the open sea in the second half of the 17th century by the construction of locks along the banks of the IJ. On the IJ side of the Damrak stood the wooden Nieuwe Brug (New Bridge). This was rebuilt in brick and stone at the end of the 17th century and given a lock. The sweet water of the outer canal was separated on both the west and east sides of the city from the salty IJ water by a brick dam. It had a gap which could be opened at ebb tide to drain excess polder water.

Rows of posts had been erected in the 16th century in the IJ as breakwaters

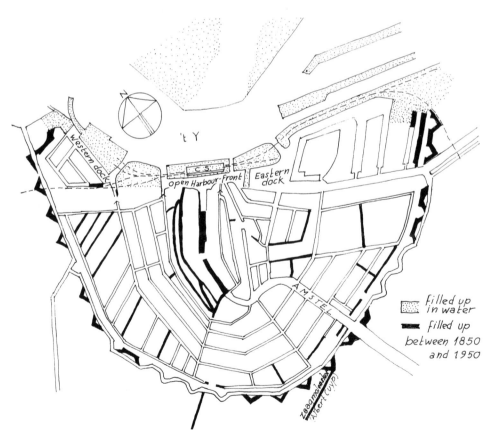

and to keep out undesirable intruders. In 1731 large numbers of ship-pile worms were suddenly discovered in the posts. These crustaceans ate large holes in the wooden posts. From then on the posts were difficult to keep in good repair.

Its unique location on the Open IJ made Amsterdam an outstanding example of a water city. Virtually all freight was carried by water through the canals, along which warehouses and merchants' homes were built. There was, however, a great problem. At the end of the 17th century the sandbank Pampus formed in the Zuiderzee. This threatened to completely close off the harbour. Ships could only sail over the obstruction at flood tide. A solution was found, thanks to the invention of the 'ships camel'. This was a sort of floating dock which could lie low or high in the water by filling it with water or pumping it empty. A full ships camel was made fast to each side of an approaching ship and then pumped empty. Ship and ships camel rose and were towed by two smaller sailing ships over the sandbank and reached the IJ. However, if the wind was blowing from the wrong direction, transport some-times had to wait days at Pampus. This gave rise to the Dutch saying: to wait at

Pampus. It means someone who is not capable of going any further, either because of too much liquor or for another reason.

Silting up continued. At the beginning of the 19th century it was decided to dig a channel from the IJ right through North Holland: the North Holland Canal. Ships were towed through by horses.

Storm tides in 1825 caused flooding in North Holland and led to increased protection for Amsterdam. The construction of a tide-free area for the city was soon begun. Dikes were built through the IJ outside the eastern and western islands. This created an open piece of water on both sides within the dikes: the Eastern Dock and the Western Dock, separated from the IJ by locks. During the building of the Western dock there was a severe setback, because the bottom was found to be unreliable. The ring dike, within which the lock had to be built, disappeared

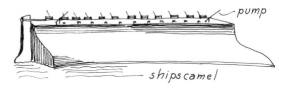

pump

shipscamel

turret called monk prevents access of undesirables

Brick water-turning wall

Shipscamels with sailing-vessel

into the depths at several places. Keeping the excavations dry was done with horse-driven mills.

The dikes narrowed the passage of the IJ so much that the increased speed of the water prevented silting. The harbour remained accessible for the largest ships through the North Holland Canal.

The IJ was closed off from the Zuiderzee around 1870 by a dam with locks. A channel was dug through the middle of the dammed off IJ from Amsterdam to the North Sea and the outer lakes were drained. The line of dunes was breached and locks were built.

The opening of the North Sea Canal led to an increase in prosperity that had an enormous effect on the city. More and more water was extracted for use in buildings and for the increasing traffic. A large number of canals were filled in during the 19th century and the first half of the 20th century, and pieces of the IJ were reclaimed for railway and harbour works.

Between 1876 and 1890 a railway line was laid on three new islands in the IJ. Central Station was built on the central island. This closed off the wide view from the city onto the IJ, although the water which remains in front of the station is still called the Open Harbour Front.

Earlier, a beginning had been made on filling in the canals in the Jordaan, not only for traffic but also to improve hygiene. The area lost many canals between 1857 and 1895, although some can still be recognized by their street names, like Rozengracht and Elandsgracht (gracht is the Dutch word for canal).

From then on canals throughout the city were filled in, at first in quick succession but after 1900 at a slower rate. In the sixties the then Police Commissioner devised a plan for filling in the Singel, the Open Harbour Front, the Lijnbaansgracht and the whole of the outer canal. Fortunately the plan was never executed.

A reclaimed piece of land took a long time to settle and, if built on, this could lead to subsidence as the new bottom pressed on the foundation piles. In the past, builders who ignored bad soil conditions in the west of the Netherlands faced enormous problems.

Dredger

← tread-wheel

Preparing the ground

Amsterdam lies on marshland with a particularly high ground water level. The ground has to be raised to make it habitable. With the expansion of the city after 1600, soil removed during the digging of new canals was used to create building plots. Soil was also removed from the old canals and the IJ with dredgers. The later part of the city expansion was more extensive and required more and better soil.

Around 1625 Amsterdam's regents acquired the right to dig sand south of Hilversum. This was brought to Amsterdam in barges along a specially created waterway. Rich Amsterdammers founded the village of 's-Graveland on the levelled ground, where they had beautiful summer houses built.

According to a regulation of 1634, sand barges could only unload at the Zand-hoek on the IJ side of the Realeneiland, one of the western islands.

The 19th century saw the arrival of all sorts of facilities, such as gas, piped water, sewers, electricity and telephone. Pipes and cables had to be laid in the ground, which necessitated a thick, clean layer of sand.

Between 1915 and 1930 sand was brought from north of the locks at IJmuiden, where the Noordersluis and the Hoogovens now stand. It was needed to build up Amsterdam South, for the Olympic Stadium among other things. After this, the need was so great that sand had to be brought from as far away as the lakes at Nederhorst den Berg, Kortenhoef and Vreeland. It was sucked up, brought to Amsterdam by ship and taken on by train. After the war, from 1945, moving sand was made much easier by vacuum pumping. Large sand vacuums sucked up sand from as much as 30 metres deep from lakes like the Sloterplas and the Vinkeveen lakes. The sand was then mixed with water and compressed over large distances to its final destination. Sand has advantages and disadvantages. The weight of the added layer of sand presses the underlying layers of peat and clay together. In addition, layers of soil press around the piles under the building. This is known as 'negative skin fiction'. The result is that the piles subside if they are not properly driven into the sand layer. The house above subsides as well. This is easy to spot in residential areas built around 1900. The long rows of façades sometimes undulate like the surface of a calm sea.

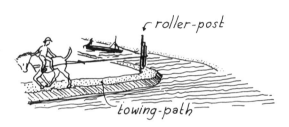

roller-post

towing-path

Transport of sand 17th c.

33

Foundations

The first houses built along the Amstel dikes were light constructions of timber with no foundations. They sank into the peat and were repeatedly being raised. The main construction of these houses consisted of posts and beams. The posts were placed in the damp ground, as a result of which the bottom part soon began to rot. Things improved in the 14th century when the wooden posts were placed on brick blocks. For brick constructions, like the castle and churches of the 13th century, it was necessary to make stronger foundations. It was impossible for the soft Amsterdam soil to carry the heavy walls. First a deep trench was dug, a little wider than the wall itself would be. Thin trunks of alder (fascines) were laid on either side of the trench. The space between the two trunks was filled with small piles of about two metres in length. Pile driving in such soft ground would have been done by hand, by two men with a heavy wooden mallet. Finally trunks were laid over the piles with more trunks laid diagonally across them. This gave a certain amount of grip, but was not much more than an improvement on the soil itself. Over this foundation lay thick oak slabs on which the wall was built.

The foundations of churches, chapels and the few brick houses of the 14th to 16th century did, however, have something close to a pile foundation, although the piles were only five to seven metres long and did not reach the

first layer of sand. These foundations also needed a deep trench, the bottom of which lay beneath ground water to prevent the wood from rotting. Two oak beams were laid along the length of the wall, about one metre apart. Beams were laid across these to create a cross-beam foundation. The small spaces between the beams were filled with pine and birch piles. They hung, as it were, in the ground, clasped by the soil. This created an irregular wooden floor on which the wall was built. In order to drive in the piles, a pile

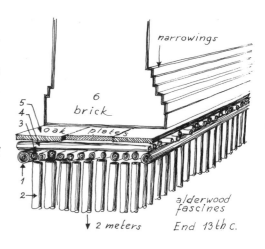

narrowings

6
brick

5
4
3

oak plates

1
2→

alderwood fascines

↓ 2 meters   End 13th c.

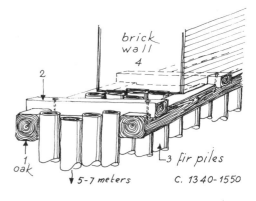

brick wall
4

2

1
oak

3 fir piles

↓ 5-7 meters   C. 1340-1550

34

driving frame was set up. At least 40 men heaved at a rope to raise the heavy ram and then let it fall onto the pile. A regular rhythm was needed for this work and the men sang. The words often reflected the rough life of the pile drivers. Here is a decent example:

> One, two, three
> Haul up the ram
> It's already May
> It's already in the ground
> There it stands straight
> Fresh and healthy.

Each pile had to enter the ground vertically, which meant that the pile driving frame constantly had to be shifted. Moving it was a real chore and it is not surprising that this job was often avoided, as a result of which not all the piles were as straight as they should have been.

There was, however, already some sort of building supervision. As early as the 15th century the city government introduced strict rules for pile driving. A law was introduced in 1503 preventing anyone from digging a new foundation on the public highway without permission from the building inspectors. The fronts of buildings had to stand neatly in a straight line. From 1528 no building activity could take place without permission from the local government. Every foundation had to be approved before building could begin.

At the beginning of the 16th century the city government granted some concessions for hiring pile driving frames of 30, 35, 38 and 40 foot (one

Amsterdam foot measures 28.3 cm.). One contractor was even given permission to keep his pile driving frame under cover on the cemetery of the Nieuwe Kerk.

A number of amazing folk stories have sprung up around the Dutch word for pile driving. One says that some buildings are built on skins, but no one has ever found a piece of leather or skin underneath an old building. The most likely cause of this old wives' tale is the way in which words were pronounced. The Dutch words for pile driving and for skins could sound similar if spoken with a mediaeval accent.

Cross-beam foundations were still being made in the 17th century, but with one important difference. The

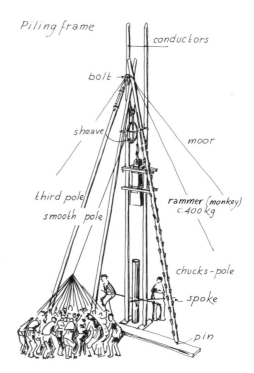

Piling frame

conductors

bolt

sheave

moor

third pole

rammer (monkey) c. 400 kg

smooth pole

chucks-pole

spoke

pin

piles now reached the first layer of sand at a depth of 13 metres. It was easy to tell when a pile had reached the full depth: once it hit the layer of sand, it could not be driven any further because this layer was impenetrable. This was called 'on stop' pile driving.

There are reports from the period that piles were not driven deep enough causing houses to subside. In some cases piles protruded above the ground water and rotted. For this reason the city government decided in 1638 that foundation timbers must lie at least half a foot under water.

Foundations from this period are much tidier than those dating from the Middle Ages. The palace on the Dam stands on 13,659 piles, which were all sawn off at the top at exactly the same level. On top of them lies a floor of planks on which the wall is built. But even then not all the problems were solved.

Foundations may be uniform but the weight they carry varies, so that one wall subsides more than another. This is easy to see at the palace in the galleries around the two inner courtyards. The lighter outer wall has subsided less than the inner walls which also carry the weight of the adjoining rooms and the roofs. Because of this, the gallery floors slope slightly inwards.

Around 1700 builders developed a new type of foundation, officially known as the Amsterdam pile foundation. For this, two rows of posts were pile driven, the weight-bearing capacity of which was worked out by rule of thumb. A cross beam was laid diagonally across each pair of posts. A tall wooden rib was laid across these beams, with a lower plank on either side. The rib was intended to prevent the wall from shifting from side to side. However, the enormous weight of the wall often pressed the heads of the piles into the cross beams, causing the planks to bend. If the ground water level dropped, the beams and the heads of the piles stood above the water and rotted. The quality of the foundations of these old buildings is therefore of continuing concern to the authorities. Through the centuries there have been problems with the Amsterdam foundations. When ornamental spires were added to a number of mediaeval towers, the foundations had to bear a greater weight. The Oude Kerk tower, built around 1300 on a fascine foundation, was given a tall open lantern of wood covered with lead in 1565. The old tower slowly sunk and

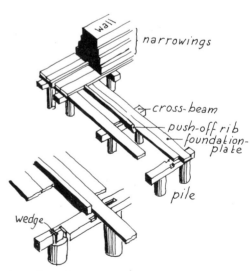

Amsterdam pile-foundation

took on an alarming tilt to the north. In 1738 piles were driven both inside and outside the tower, on to which a brick casing was built. The old tower hangs inside this. Since then, however, the old tower has subsided a few centimetres inside its casing. The tower was also supported by high walls on the north and south side, but these were removed during the restoration of the church in 1960.

The Montelbaanstoren, built on marsh, was given an ornamental spire in 1606, but the weight proved too much. Four years later the tower suddenly began to

lean. With a great deal of difficulty and the help of the local population, the giant was heaved upright, the foundations strengthened and the tower bricked around. The reinforced foot is still there.

When Central Station was built in 1886, another problem arose. The bottom of the IJ is worn away to a depth of about 24 metres. The upper layer of sand has disappeared. The depth made it necessary to drive two wooden piles on top of each other, held together by a hollow pipe. Around 8,700 piles support this building.

When the new Exchange was built on the reclaimed part of the Damrak, Amsterdam Council skimped on the foundations, much against the wishes of the architect Berlage. The foundations used 4,780 thirteen-metre piles and 100 ten-metre piles. The soft, new land sank under the weight of the new building and took the pile foundations with it. The building had already subsided and the walls cracked by the time it opened. By 1909 structural alterations had been done, such as smaller brick arches under the support point in the large arches of the Merchandise Exchange. Extensive repair work to the foundations was carried out in 1960.

Concrete piles have been almost exclusively used since the Second World War. These do not rot and can carry a greater weight. More modern pile driving frames and rams, driven by explosions of diesel oil, also made their appearance. As a result, piles have become longer and buildings taller. To date, the longest piles are under the

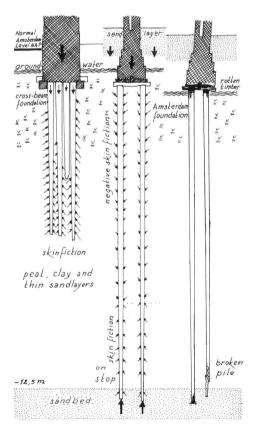

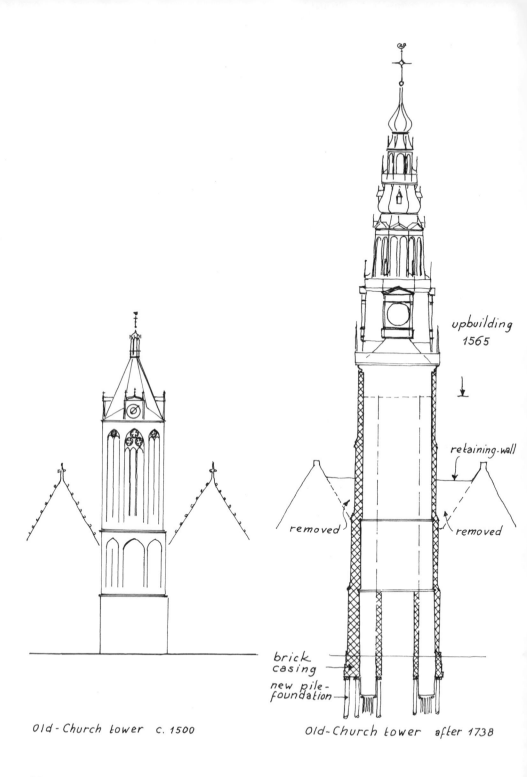

upbuilding
1565

retaining-wall

removed

removed

brick
casing
new pile-
foundation

Old-Church tower c. 1500

Old-Church tower after 1738

Netherlands Bank on the Frederiksplein. Earlier buildings on this spot had 13 metre piles to the first layer of sand. The present 74 metres tall building built in 1967 stands on 21 metre concrete piles reaching the second layer of sand. The so-called Satellite, built in 1989 and 65 metres tall, has eight 63 metre concrete piles which were constructed in the ground and reach into the third layer of sand.

Pile driving is impossible inside existing buildings for improving or reinforcing foundations. Piles have to be pushed into the ground. These are usually concrete tubes set one above the other. The soil under the pile is re;moved with a pulse: an iron tube with a lid that can be slid inside the concrete tube. As the pulse is pulled up, the lid shuts automatically and takes the soil from under the pile with it. Amsterdammers have always had to be inventive when it comes to building on their soft ground.

The timber trade

In the west of The Netherlands, timber was always imported because of the lack of forests. Logs were floated on the tides down the rivers Rhine and Maas to the city of Dordrecht, where they were traded. There was also a lively timber trade in Deventer on the IJssel. As early as the 14th century large-scale timber sawing took place in Amsterdam for smaller pieces such as planks, ribs, slats and wainscot. A beam was laid on two trestles and sawn lengthways by two men with a frame-saw. The sawyers had their own guild; anyone who did not live in the city was not allowed to ply the trade.

People came to Amsterdam from far and near, even from Flanders, to buy cut wood for buildings and ships. Timber was stored along the banks and inland terrain of the IJ (houttuinen is Dutch for timber yards) and the canals. Many street names reflect this: the Joden Houttuinen along the Hout-kopers (timber merchants) Burgwal, Rechtboomsloot (straight tree canal), Kromboomsloot (twisted tree canal). The city hall/music theatre now stands on the former Houtgracht and Houtstraat.

The growth of the city made it necessary to move the timber markets, but for ease of transportation they remained along the water. Timber wharves also disappeared from the old centre to the newly created islands in the IJ.

Until around 1600, the main timber used in the Netherlands was oak from Germany and Belgium. For ship-building, too, large quantities of wood were needed, mainly oak bentwood. This was also used for trusses.

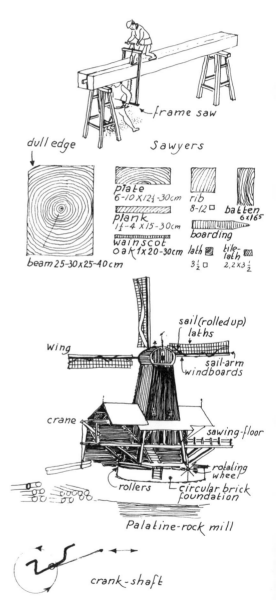

frame saw

Sawyers

dull edge

plate 6-10 x 12¼-30cm   rib   8-12 □   batten 6x16.5

plank 1¼-4 x 15-30cm   boarding

wainscot oak 1x20-30cm   lath   tile-lath

beam 25-30x25-40cm   3½ □   2,2x3½

sail (rolled up) laths

wing

sail-arm windboards

crane

sawing-floor

rotating wheel

rollers   circular brick foundation

Palatine-rock mill

crank-shaft

After 1600 pine was imported from Scandinavia and the Baltic countries. Pine for use as piles was floated along the Rhine and the Maas. Three types of pine were used in the Netherlands: silver spruce known as 'Tanne' in German-speaking areas, rough pine known as 'furu' in Scandinavia and fine pine known as 'granen' in the North. Around 1600 the two Scandinavian words were reversed by Dutch timber merchants.

Cut timber was sold to Amsterdam measurements. Before 1820 the most important of these were the thumb (for the width) and the foot (for the length). These measurements vary from place to place. In Amsterdam a thumb was roughly the same as elsewhere, but the foot was just 11 thumbs long instead of the more usual 12. This made the prices charged by the Amsterdam timber merchants appear lower than those of the competition. Amsterdammers also thought themselves clever when it came to sawmills. Around 1600 the first crank shaft was introduced in a sawmill in the Zaanstreek. This made it possible to change a circular movement into a back-and-forth swing. The revolving cogs, driven by the sails of the mill, altered to a sawing motion. Sawing timber with wind power is cheaper than by hand. The Amsterdam sawyers and timber merchants faced stiff competition from the Zaanstreek (north-west of Amsterdam), where cheaper pine was the order of the day. The Amsterdam trade relied mainly on oak. After a while Amsterdam city government took protective measures. From then on it

was forbidden to transport uncut timber through the waterways of Amsterdam. The rafts and ships from Dordrecht and Deventer could no longer sail along the IJ to the Zaan. In addition, no timber which was not cut in the city could be traded at the Amsterdam timber auctions.

Of course the Zaanstreek found other routes for transporting timber. On the edge of Amsterdam, particularly to the west of the city, sawmills gradually appeared, but by then the tide had already turned in favour of the Zaanstreek. The sawyers guild was disbanded and the timber trade became less important. Even sawyers with a mill outside the city walls but with offices in the city were not allowed to sell uncut timber, as that would be at the expense of the municipal timber merchants!

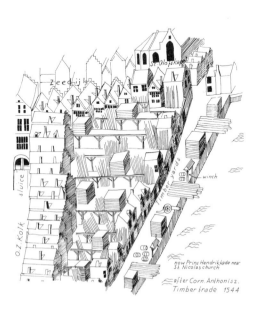

now Prins Hendrikkade near St. Nicolas church

after Corn. Anthonisz.
Timber trade 1544

Crafts and building materials

Everyone working in the building trade was a member of one of the various guilds, which mainly represented more than one trade. No one was allowed to do the work of another trade, not even within the same guild. Carpenters, for example, in the St. Joseph guild were not allowed to make wainscotting or furniture. This was done by cabinet makers.

Carpenters were always the most important craftsmen in Amsterdam, where houses and large buildings were constructed mainly from timber. There is a stone tablet along the Egelantiersgracht in the Jordaan which shows the guild examination of a young carpenter. He is using an axe to hew a regulation size beam into a rectangle, from which he must make a cross-bar window-frame.

From the end of the 12th century Dutch bricks were fired from clay. The largest brick is still called a 'cloister brick' after the important part played by monks in its firing. The oldest bricks, from the 13th century, were used for the castle and the Oude Kerk. They are roughly 30 cm long and 6.5 cm thick. Over the centuries the bricks in the west of the Netherlands became gradually smaller. The size was also dependent on the type of clay available from different areas. The colour was determined by the composition of the clay in a particular area. The soil along the Old Rhine between Woerden and Leiden contained a lot of iron and the bricks were a pretty orange-red. The clay along the Dutch IJssel at Gouda contained more lime and the bricks were yellow. Grey and faintly purple

The young carpenter
Stone tablet Egelantiersgracht 15

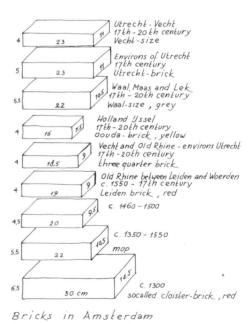

Bricks in Amsterdam

bricks came from the clay along the great rivers and the Utrechtse Vecht. Very even bricks came from the Vecht area in the 18th century, perfect for laying nice trim façades. These were widely used in Amsterdam.

Around the same time, the firing process was improved and produced harder bricks known as 'clinkers' because of the metallic sound they gave when tapped together. Clinkers prevent rising damp provided they are anchored with a waterproof cement mortar. Since the 16th century ground tuff stone has been used under the name 'trass'. This is why the watertight strip is still known as the damp proof 'trass course'. Portland cement – now known just as cement – has been in production since the second half of the 19th century. Mortar was mainly mixed from lime which was produced by firing shells from the coastal areas of the North Sea and the Zuiderzee. Bricklayers also laid floor tiles, not only glazed flagstones but also natural stone, mainly black Belgian limestone and white Italian marble. They also tiled the famous glazed white wall tiles, which were often decorated in blue, purple or other colours.

The Netherlands has no native stone suitable for building. As early as the Middle Ages natural stone was being transported by water. Varieties of blue hardstone and white limestone were brought from Belgium along the rivers Maas and Schelde. Ships brought vulcanic rock like tuff stone, basalt and trachyte from Germany along the Rhine. And from around 1450, sandstone was brought from Bentheim along the Overijsselse Vecht and the Zuiderzee. From the end of the 16th century natural stone was imported by sea, such as sandstone from the Wezer area in Germany. This was loaded into ships in Bremen. Light red limestone from the Swedish island of Öland was imported as ballast in timber-carrying ships, and used mainly as floor tiles. There is an example in the entrance to the Burgerweeshuis (City Orphanage) off the Kalverstraat and in the palace on the Dam. Italian marbles were used for floors, walls and chimneys but were very expensive.

The construction of the railway in the 19th century enriched the assortment of imported stone: volcanic rocks like granite and diabas from Bavaria, shell limestone from North Bavaria and granite from Scandinavia.

The fashion in the 15th century was to intersperse rows of bricks at regular intervals with a row of white Belgian natural stone, known as 'Gobertanger'. This is known as 'bacon layers' because the effect is of a rasher of bacon with its strips of red meat and white fat. The effect disappeared when sandstone was used instead of natural stone. Sandstone is pale yellow but weathers into grey. Sometimes 'bacon layers' were created by painting the sandstone pale yellow. Bricks were quickly damaged by salt water. This is why the lower part of the city wall along the Geldersekade, which was exposed to the tides, was built from Bentheim sandstone. Many pieces of the quay wall still bear witness to this. The last bastion on the north west side of the 17th century city wall stood in the IJ. It was called Blauw Hoofd

(Blue Head) because it was built out of blue hardstone.

Stone masons of the late-Middle Ages often left their mark on their work. One of these marks can be seen on the Mirakelkolom (Miracle Column) on Rokin, the remains of the Holy Place or Nieuwezijds Chapel.

Hard wearing lead and slate were essential for building, despite their high price. Slaters covered the roofs of important buildings with slates; thin slabs of grey-blue natural stone. Corners, ridges and gutters were protected with lead sheeting. The indispensible drainpipes and the pumps inside the houses were also fitted by plumbers.

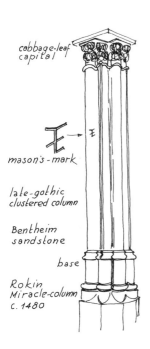

cabbage-leaf capital

mason's-mark

late-gothic clustered column

Bentheim sandstone

base

Rokin Miracle-column c. 1480

Soldering was done with a mixture of lead and tin, which was melted with red hot soldering irons so that it flowed into the joins and fixed the lead pieces firmly together. Soldering irons were heated in a pot of fire and it was strictly forbidden to take the pot onto the roof. A plumber always had loose handles wrapped in rope with him for carrying the soldering irons up to the roof. There is an illustration of this over the guild doorway of the Waag on the Nieuwmarkt. Sometimes a plumber wanted to save time and took the fire pot onto the roof. This is how the fire in the Nieuwe Kerk of 1645 began.

Cramps, nails, railings, stoop rails, bars and similar objects were beaten from iron by the smith.

Nails were hand beaten and very expensive. After the industrial revolution around 1830, they were made of thick iron threads. The Dutch call these 'thread nails'. These were much cheaper and as a result more timber was nailed together instead of the labour intensive mortise and tenon and dovetail joints.

Iron can also be cast in moulds for making things like ornamental stoop balusters, grates and cramp rosettes. In the 19th century large building components like church windows and warehouse columns, were also made from cast iron.

Enormous iron and steel constructions were built, like the roofs of Central Station and the Berlage Exchange. Timber was pushed into the back-ground as a building material.

Masonry

To build a wall, a mason uses bricks and mortar. In earliest times mortar was made by mixing lime and sand with water. These days cement is also added. The mortar is spread between the bricks, where it hardens. Bricks and mortar form a strong construction. The length or stretch of a brick is twice as long as its width or head. The thickness is about half that of the head. The bricks are laid in bonds. The vertical lines of mortar must never lie directly above each other, as this can cause cracking. Corners are formed with a quarter brick (a closer) or three quarter brick (a three-quarter). Corners were made with closers before around 1700 and have a particular look. From then on small bricks were considered unwieldy and three-quarters were laid along the length. The stretchers in succeeding layers can be laid straight on top of each other. This is called 'English bond'. They can also jump half a brick which creates small crosses in the wall, the 'cross bond'.

Bricks are heavy. It is necessary to have an arch or a stretch above a window opening in order to carry most of the weight. In the late-Middle Ages arches were usually tall and pointed. During the Renaissance the preference was for shallower arches. A stretch or Dutch arch is used as a sort of wide wedge, set fast in the opening to prevent pressure on the underlying woodwork. To do

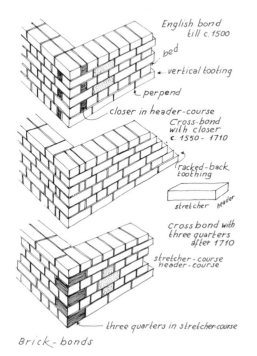

English bond
till c. 1500
bed
vertical tooling
perpend
closer in header-course
Cross-bond
with closer
c. 1550 - 1710
racked-back
toothing
stretcher   header
cross bond with
three quarters
after 1710
stretcher - course
header - course
three quarters in stretcher-course

Brick - bonds

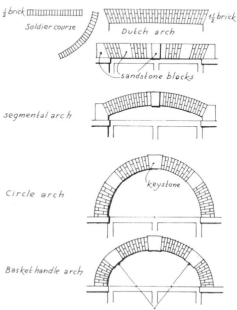

½ brick
Soldier course
Dutch arch
1½ brick
sandstone blocks
segmental arch
Circle arch
keystone
Basket handle arch

45

this neatly, all the bricks on all sides must be cut at an angle, a precise skill. The rigid lines which dominated architecture from the Classical period onwards did not lend themselves to arches. They needed stretches. A soldier course – a row of bricks laid on their sides – was used above a small opening, under a window frame, to cover a clock gable or on a separate piece of wall. Particularly noteworthy is 17th century red brickwork of exceptionally smooth bricks and with no visible pointing. Leiden bricks were used for this, individually cut and ground to size by the mason, giving an even rectangle with very sharp sides. The back was cut at an angle. At the front these bricks are laid 'cold' on each other, but a lot of mortar was used between the bricks at the back. Sometimes a wall was built with contours or even to give the

illusion of perspective. These tours de force were tests for masons and won them the title of master mason in the Saint Barbara guild.

Most of the pointing is neatly finished. From the Middle Ages until in the 17th century, the mortar was finished directly after bricklaying. In the 18th century the very rigid bricks used for the façades demanded high quality pointing. A very thin slat (feather) was laid on the outer edge of a row of bricks. The next row of bricks was then laid. Once the mortar had hardened, the feather was pulled out and the groove neatly pointed. Very little mortar can be seen in some of these vertical joins.

The 19th century saw the arrival of machine-made bricks and in general pointing became thicker again. Fantasy pointing arrived in the 20th century. This sometimes lies as much as a centimetre behind the surface of the façade. It is certainly decorative, but it lets a lot more rainwater through the wall.

Bentheim sandstone

soldering iron
slater's hammer

handle wrapped in cord
plumbers spoon
soldering iron
plumbers iron
slaters cutting iron
chalk-line

Masons tools

Bricklayers tools

chip chisel
mallet
scotch
plumb-rule
chisels
level
pointing-trowel
square
bevel
pan-iron
dividers
darby
trowel

Weigh-house Nieuwmarkt Barbara-guild doorway

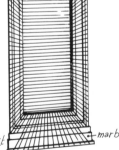

masters test
Weigh-house Nieuwmarkt

marbel

46

Cramps

There are often oblongs or rosettes made of iron on façades. These are the cramps which fix beams to the outer wall. They prevent the wall from bulging. Thin walls were fastened to the timber frame, the beams and the roof. Gables are also anchored in this way. Tall chimneys and the section of the top gable above the ridge are usually anchored to the roof ridge. A regulation of 1669 specified that every other beam must have an 'appropriate cramp'. Two beams had to be fastened together with a coupling iron, so they could not slide apart.

Façade cramps usually consist of two pieces. The simplest have a straight rod and a hammered piece which is nailed to the beam inside the wall, with a wrought iron eye on the outside. This creates a vertical 'slot bolt' with a beaten ridge to prevent sagging. Sometimes the smith has added a symbol to the slot bolt in the form of a diagonal cross between two horizontal lines or another motif. Amsterdam cramps from the 16th and 17th centuries were sometimes given wrought iron ornaments, but not as often as in other cities.

The disadvantage of iron is that it can rust and rust has a volume seven times greater than that of the iron itself. It therefore cracks the surrounding brickwork. To solve this problem, the hot cramps were oiled or tarred immediately after being beaten. Iron was also wrapped in hessian, thus creating sufficient space for any subsequent increase in volume. Cramps looked out of place in the precise brickwork of the 18th century. Hidden cramps were therefore used, covered by the brickwork. If these rust, a bump forms in the façade. Around 1850 cramps were made with a cast iron rosette or other decoration, and were fixed to the façade by a nut. At the beginning of the 20th century there were even Jugendstil cramps made from wrought iron.

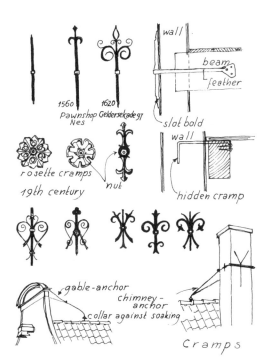

1560
Pawnshop
Nes

1620
Geldersekade 97

wall
beam
feather

slot bold

rosette cramps
19th century

nut

wall

hidden cramp

gable-anchor
chimney-anchor
collar against soaking

Cramps

Timber frames

The oldest houses had a frame of oak posts and beams, joined together by mortise and tenon and fastened with wooden nails. Walls and floors were nailed to the frame. The corner between beam and post was a weak point and was therefore supported with a bent piece of wood (a curved brace) and strengthened with a sole plate. Together, the two posts, the beam, the curved brace and the sole plate form a truss. To build a house, a number of trusses were placed one behind the other; initially at a distance of about three metres. They were brought closer together in the 16th century. That was also when the braces in Amsterdam houses often curved in such a way that they were known as a swan's neck. Churches also had this sort of frame. Thick beams with wall posts and curved braces criss-cross the spaces high above the ground.

The city government kept a close eye on the building of timber frames. If a carpenter made the posts of the trusses shorter than ordered, he was not allowed to add an extra length of wood but had to start again. These had to be supported on projections from the wall (corbels).

Once a truss had been put together, it was raised upright with the help of a crane. Cranes had been in use for centuries to move heavy loads like stone and timber. A contractor without a crane could hire one from the guild of carpenters. The price was determined by the weight of the load. A beam measuring 30 x 30 cm in diameter cost five cents; a thicker beam cost ten cents. Window frames, façade beams and roof sections each had their price. At the end of the 16th century the price was determined by the height of the crane. These were between 3,5 and seven metres tall.

Wood is very flexible and adjusted much better than brick walls to the distortions caused by the soft soil. But fire regulations made it necessary to build thin brick outer walls and chimneys, although floors and roofs still rested on a timber frame. Posts were partly concealed in the walls (wall posts) and in the mid-17th century wall posts and curved braces disappeared completely.

When attic space was brought into use, more room was needed under the roof beams. It had to be possible to walk under the beams with a load on the shoulders without banging against them. The base of the roof was therefore raised about one metre above the attic beams. The short wall under the roof base was called a parapet after the defensive walls of castles and cities. This alteration added a new word to the Dutch language. The Dutch word for making something deeper is 'verdiepen' and this new space was a 'verdieping', a word which has come to mean 'storey'.

More and more storeys were added. As early as the 15th century space was increased by adding a floor to the bottom trusses. Later on, as many as four storeys were placed one above the other.

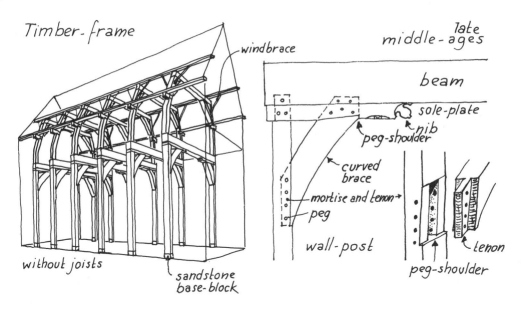

Timber-frame

late middle-ages

windbrace

beam

sole-plate

nib

peg-shoulder

curved brace

mortise and tenon

peg

wall-post

tenon

peg-shoulder

without joists

sandstone base-block

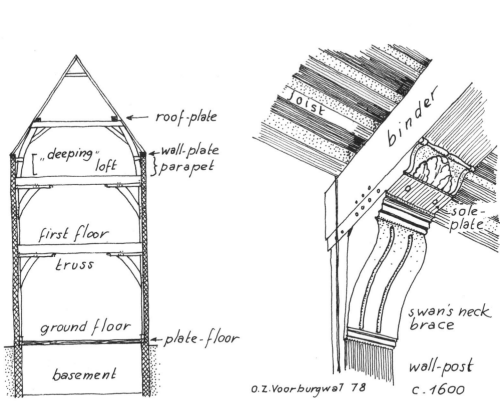

roof-plate

"deeping" loft

wall-plate parapet

first floor

truss

ground floor

plate-floor

basement

joist

binder

sole-plate

swan's neck brace

wall-post c.1600

O.Z.Voorburgwal 78

49

Joists

The distance of three metres, which until 1550 was the usual distance between floor beams and truss posts, was too wide to be bridged in one go with floorboards. Oak ribs with a cross-section of 10 x 10 cm and placed about 30 cm apart were used to fill the gap. At first these were called beams and ribs but in the 19th century they were given the name 'mother-and-child-beams'. They have not been made since the mid-17th century.

Seen from below, the seams between the floorboards looked ugly. They also allowed dust to fall through. In important rooms this problem was solved by lining the ribs with very thin, handsawn oak (lining wainscot).

In some of the raised areas of the city, along the old sea dike for example, a sort of cellar was created under the house. There was, however, little space between the ground floor and the ground water. The ceiling of the cellar had to be as thin as possible and was made from 8 cm thick timber sheets.

Beams were laid much closer together around 1600, usually with less than a metre between them. Along the wall they often rested on a wooden console. The floorboards were grooved along their length, into which went a very thin, narrow slat (a feather) so that the boards fitted snugly. This also prevented dust from falling through the seams.

The feather later made way for tongue and groove.

Floor beams from this period were usually made from pine, because oak had become difficult to obtain and therefore expensive. Until the mid-17th century oak beams and ribs were only made for the most important rooms. From then on these rooms had panelling under their beams. These panels were usually painted. In the 18th century the sharp lower edges of the beams were often shaved into a rounded bead contour.

In many houses the wooden floor carries a layer of natural stone tiles, white and black marble or red Swedish Öland stone. Between the wood and stone floors is a thick layer of shells, fossilized through years of pressure. These floors can often be seen in paintings from the Golden Age.

Around 1700 Italian stucco workers began arriving in the Netherlands. They created richly ornamented stucco ceilings. Laths were nailed under the beams and a layer of thatch added, held in place with copper thread. The thatch was treated with lime mortar which soaked in and acted like glue. The next layer had plaster and cow hair worked into it. Plaster swells as it hardens which made the layer stick fast. Hair ensures that the mortar layer stays firmly in place. Beautiful ornaments were often created on the final layer. Walls in halls, stairways and rooms were also given this type of stucco decoration, which is typical of the styles from Louis XIV onwards.

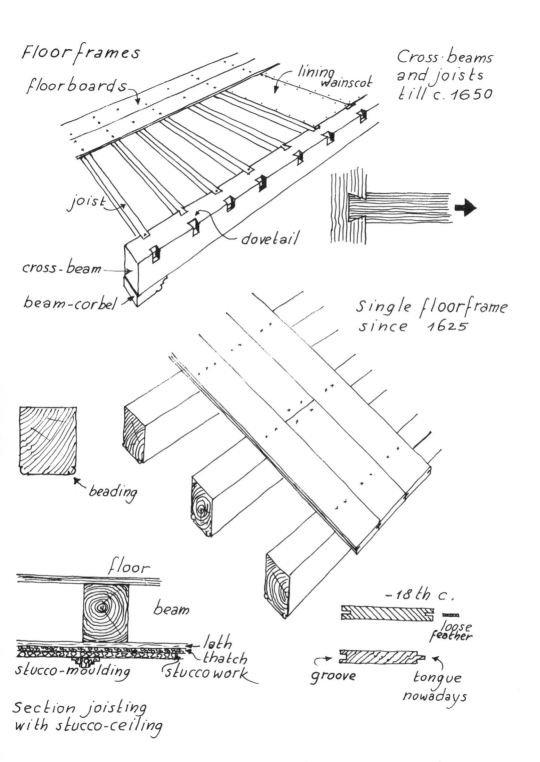

Floor frames

floorboards

lining
wainscot

Cross-beams
and joists
till c. 1650

joist

dovetail

cross-beam

beam-corbel

Single floorframe
since 1625

beading

floor

beam

lath
thatch
stuccowork

stucco-moulding

Section joisting
with stucco-ceiling

−18th c.

loose
feather

groove

tongue
nowadays

51

Roofs

Early roofs were usually constructed from thin tree trunks or oak ribs (rafters) set at an angle. A horizontal collar was fitted to each pair of rafters under the ridge. Tile laths were nailed to the rafters, over which roof tiles were laid. The tiles were visible from inside and they often leaked if it rained or snowed. Horizontal beams or roof plates supported the rafters. An attic above these roof plates was called a roof plate attic. The trusses stood at right angles to the length of the roof on loft beams and carried the roof plates. Until shortly after 1600 the legs of the trusses were nearly always of bent oak. Wall plates rested on sole pieces which protruded horizontally from the truss legs. On top of these rested the rafters. As soon as the trusses and rafters were

in place, the side walls (first of wood and later of brick) were extended one metre above the attic floor.

About ten late-mediaeval roofs have been preserved in Amsterdam. The Oude Kerk still has all its mediaeval roofs, dating from various periods between 1300 and 1600. This gives it more mediaeval roofs than any other building in the Netherlands. Another special feature of these roofs is the vaulted ceiling, which creates soaring spaces high above the top of the church walls. These timber wagon vaults give the illusion of an upturned ship. But of course the ceiling is made from very thin planks and could not possibly withstand the heavy pressure of water. These timber wagon vault ceilings were not only constructed in the Middle Ages, but are also found in the new reformed churches of the 17th century. Shortly after 1600 building was begun on a series of warehouses to store the

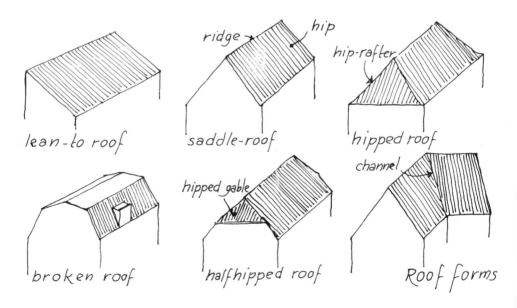

lean-to roof saddle-roof hipped roof broken roof halfhipped roof Roof forms

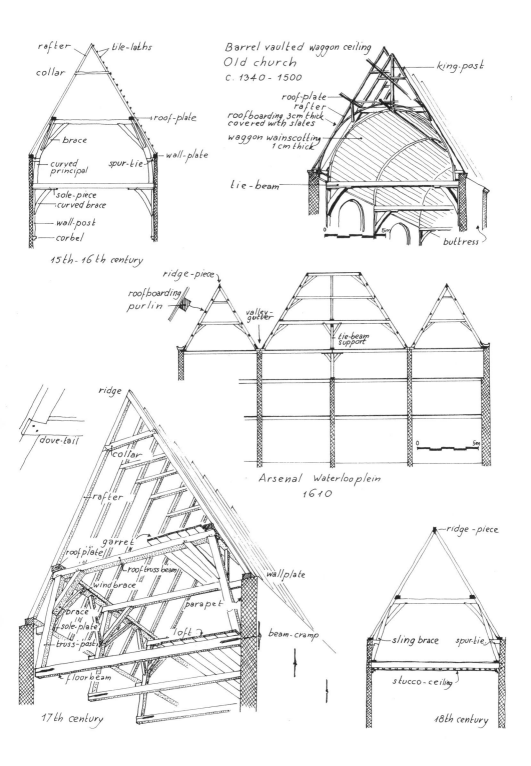

rafter — tile-laths

collar

roof-plate

brace

curved principal   spur-tie   wall-plate

sole-piece
curved brace

wall-post

corbel

15th - 16th century

Barrel vaulted waggon ceiling
Old church
c. 1340 - 1500

king-post

roof-plate
rafter
roofboarding 3cm thick covered with slates
waggon wainscotting 1 cm thick

tie-beam

buttress

0   5m

ridge-piece

roofboarding
purlin

valley-gutter

tie-beam support

Arsenal Waterlooplein
1610

0   5m

dove-tail

ridge

collar

rafter

garret
roof-plate
roof truss beam
wind brace

brace
sole-plate
truss-post

floorbeam

17th century

wallplate

parapet

loft

beam-cramp

ridge-piece

sling brace   spur-tie

stucco-ceiling

18th century

53

peat which was shared out amongst the poor. This complex, later known as the Arsenaal on the Waterlooplein and now opposite the Stopera, had to be absolutely watertight, otherwise the peat would swell and the building literally burst apart. Watertight roof boarding had to be laid over the rafters. The carpenters used purlins. These were let into the trusses with two sides lying in the slope of the roof. Roof boarding was nailed to these. This type of roof was uncommon for another reason: it was the first large roof in Amsterdam to be made entirely from pine. Purlin roofs later became the general rule and traditional roofs in the Netherlands are still constructed in this way.

In the wet and windy Netherlands the usual pitch for roofs is between 50 and 60 degrees. This gives good drainage for rain water. Flatter roofs have to be covered with metal leaf, but this could only be done after the introduction of zinc in the 19th century. Only then were these roofs really effective and affordable. These days a roof can be totally flat, as long as it is treated with a layer of tar or bitumen.

Most of the roofs of houses in the city centre stand at right angles to the façades. There are only a few buildings where the roof runs parallel to the street. For example, shallow coach houses in the streets between the canals and wide buildings without top gables. Roofs can appear very different, depending on the shape and the construction of the roof areas or hips. The simplest roof slopes on one side and is called a lean-to roof. A roof over a building with two sloping hips leaning against each other is a saddle roof. A slanting end, the bottom part of which lies higher than the guttering on the side, is known as a hipped gable. Where there is a sloping roof on four sides of a square building, it is called a hipped roof. The 17th century French architect Mansart made much use of varying roof pitches and these are known as mansard roofs. They were only introduced into the Netherlands in the 19th century.

Roofing

The first houses had thatched roofs, a distinct fire hazard in the city. In the 15th century some important buildings were roofed with slate and more expensive houses with tiles. At the end of the 15th century tilemakers introduced a new model: a wavy, flat piece of fired clay. The upper curve (the nose) on one side fitted over the shallower curve on the other side, enabling them to be fitted together. On most old Dutch roof tiles the nose fits the next tile to the right. This is known as covering to the right. The tiles are made by hand and never fit very well. In some places, where the south-west wind can blow rain through the gaps, tiles covering to the left were used. The top of the roof was closed with special ridge tiles.

Tiles were originally laid without roof boarding. To keep out snow and rain they were sealed with lime mortar, sometimes containing cow hair to prevent it from falling out when it shrank.

Most roof tiles are red, the colour of the iron-compound they contain. If the oven is closed at the end of the firing process, lack of oxygen causes the red iron-compound to turn black. The tiles are then grey and are called 'braised' tiles. Although red tiles can last for centuries, grey tiles are more weather resistant.

Tile manufacturers went over to steam machines in the 19th century. This meant that straighter and more waterproof tiles could be produced. Slates came from abroad. Scale-shaped slates from the Rhine area were nailed down in upward sloping rows. Very thin rectangular roof slates were brought from quarries along the river Maas on the Belgian and French borders. These were laid in horizontal rows.

Lead is expensive. It is used to cover parts of towers, but it does create problems when used to cover large areas of a roof. As a result, this is seldom seen. But ridges, gutters and joins on pitched roofs are often covered with lead, which weathers to a silver-grey.

Copper is even more expensive and was also very difficult to make in thin sheets. The coppersmith had to beat the new copper for a long time to achieve a thickness of around one millimetre. Only exceptional buildings were roofed with copper. It was also used for weather vanes and the hands of clocks on towers. Copper is often gilded with a very thin layer of real gold, and weather vanes on the tops of towers treated in this way glitter in the sun. But if it is not varnished, it turns green. Manufacture of zinc sheeting began in the 19th century. This was a lot cheaper and offered many possibilities for roofing and decoration. Important 19th century buildings are notable for their richly decorated zinc cornices.

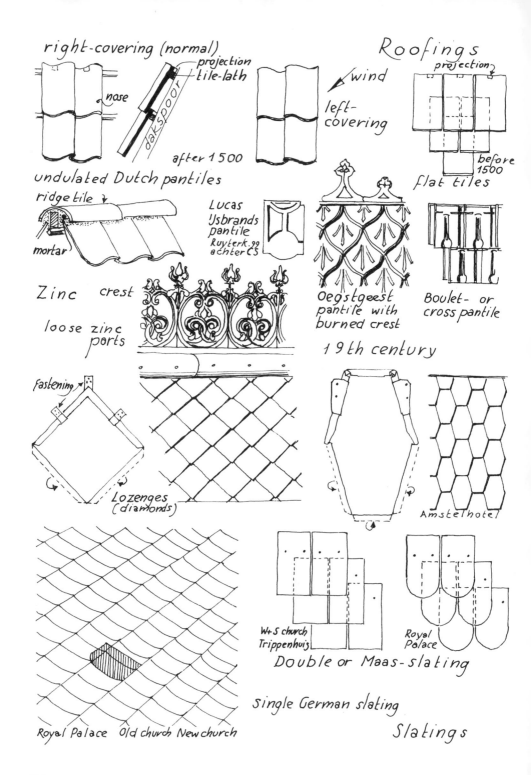

right-covering (normal)

projection
tile-lath
nose
dakspoor

after 1500

undulated Dutch pantiles

Roofings

projection

wind

left-covering

before 1500

flat tiles

ridge tile
mortar

Lucas
IJsbrands
pantile
Ruyterk. 99
achter CS

Oegstgeest
pantile with
burned crest

Boulet- or
cross pantile

Zinc   crest

loose zinc
parts

19th century

fastening

Lozenges
(diamonds)

Amstelhotel

W + S church
Trippenhuis

Royal
Palace

Double or Maas-slating

single German slating

Royal Palace   Old church New church

Slatings

Façades and gables

The front façades of late-mediaeval timber houses consisted of a timber lower front, above which each storey protruded about 20 cm from the one below. This avoided the need for complicated timber joints between each storey and allowed rainwater to drip off each section. This can still be seen on the timber house at the beginning of the Zeedijk.

When side walls had to be of brick in the mid-15th century, front walls, too, were built from brick, although the lower front remained of timber. Timber façades could still be built. However, where brick was used the sections could no longer protrude. This led to a loss of space, so façades were built 'in flight', with the front façade leaning slightly forward. A wall built straight up is 'in line', that is to say following the line of the plumb-line. A regulation from 1565 stipulated that a façade was not allowed to lean forward more than 2.5 cm per metre. Corner houses were built 'in flight' on two sides. Back walls are nearly always 'in line'.

As well as winning space, an 'in flight' façade offers other advantages. Rainwater that penetrates the brickwork, flows out again and drips from the cornices which still accentuate each floor. In addition, hoisting goods is not impeded by the wall. The façade even looks better. Where a modern façade is built 'in line' between a row of 'in flight' façades, it looks as if it is leaning backwards.

Draining rainwater from the outside of the façade has always been important. Dirt does not run down the wall, woodwork does not rot as much and as little damp as possible is let through the thin wall of the façade. Most façades were therefore given a row of crossed sandstone slabs or soldier-courses. Windows have protruding sills of natural stone and a strip of lead on the frames. In addition, a strip of lead was

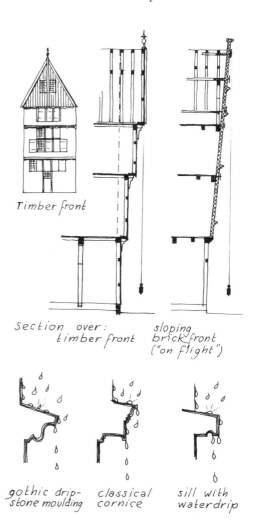

Timber front

Section over:
timber front

sloping brick front ("on flight")

gothic drip-stone moulding

classical cornice

sill with waterdrip

built into every storey across the complete width to drain water out of the brickwork. Unfortunately modern architects have forgotten the usefulness of cornices and leave them off. Result: dirty façades and damaged brickwork. Most houses in the old city centre stand with their narrow side on the street. There are usually three windows along the width of the front façade, some-times two or four. Houses on double plots usually had an entrance in the middle and five windows along the width.

A house with its narrow side on the street needs a way of closing the roof. This is the gable. Old timber houses just had a simple triangle. But it is difficult to close off a brick façade and a pitched roof line. The easiest way is to give the gable two oblong 'shoulders'. To do this, the sloping side at the top is finished with a soldier-course and the top reshaped into a rectangle. This 'triangular gable' was sometimes covered with natural stone and given a pediment and statuary.

The step gable, built like a flight of steps on two sides, was the most common form in the 17th century. The steps are covered with sandstone slabs. Right on the top is a narrow brick pilaster on which stands a sandstone ball, vase or lion. A step gable requires good maintenance because of the many places where wind and rain can cause damage.

Later in the 17th century, gables were given an oblong shape: the neck gable. These do not close the whole roof gap and have a hewed sandstone piece on either side: a croll stone. Stonecutters provided these from stock, made for standard gables of 18 and 20 foot (5 and 5.65 m). If they did not fit well, they had to be cut to fit or a separate curl or vase was added. There is a special form of neck gable that has a small extra storey with its own croll stones: a raised neck gable.

Gables were also made in the form of a bell in many varieties: the bell gable. The hollow line nearly touched the edge of the roof. The simple gable was covered with a soldier-course and a rounded top roofing and enlivened with two sandstone curls on the bottom, often in Louis XV style. The wide façades of the large canal houses were usually covered hori-zontally, because the roof ran parallel to

crest
hoist beam
gable-coping sandstone
hoist-doors
spring-volute
Dutch arch
sash-window
lead strip
sill blue stone
baluster
stoop
basement-entry
pile foundation
bell-shaped gable
hidden cramp
roof gutter
floor joists
beam-cramps
entrance upstairs house

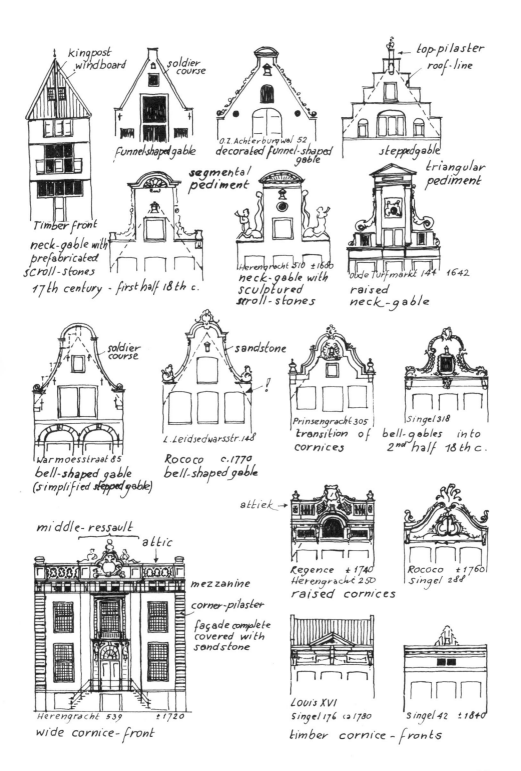

kingpost
windboard

soldier
course

Funnel-shaped gable

O.Z. Achterburgwal 52
decorated funnel-shaped
gable

top-pilaster
roof-line

stepped gable

Timber front

neck-gable with
prefabricated
scroll-stones

17th century - first half 18th c.

segmental pediment

Herengracht 510 ±1600
neck-gable with
sculptured
scroll-stones

triangular pediment

Oude Turfmarkt 144 1642
raised
neck-gable

soldier
course

Warmoesstraat 85
bell-shaped gable
(simplified stepped gable)

sandstone

L.Leidsedwarsstr.148
Rococo c.1770
bell-shaped gable

Prinsengracht 305
transition of
cornices

Singel 318
bell-gables into
2nd half 18th c.

middle-ressault

attic

attiek →

mezzanine

corner-pilaster

façade complete
covered with
sandstone

Herengracht 539   ±1720
wide cornice-front

Regence ±1740
Herengracht 250
raised cornices

Rococo ±1760
Singel 288

Louis XVI
Singel 176 ca 1780

Singel 42 ±1840

timber cornice-fronts

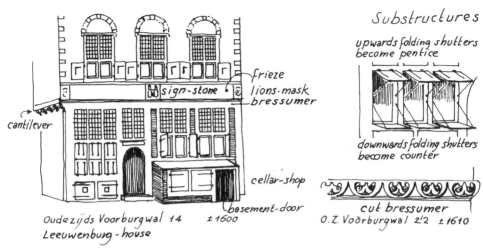

frieze
lions-mask
bressumer
sign-stone

cantilever

cellar-shop

basement-door

Oudezijds Voorburgwal 14 ±1600
Leeuwenburg-house

Substructures

upwards folding shutters
become pentice

downwards folding shutters
become counter

cut bressumer
O.Z. Voorburgwal 22 ±1610

entersole

De Eendracht St.Petrus St.Jan   Wapen van
               NoachsArck   Alssendelft

Zandhoek 2-7 · Built 1657-1660, modernized 18th - 19th centuries
Bressumers and posts being maintained

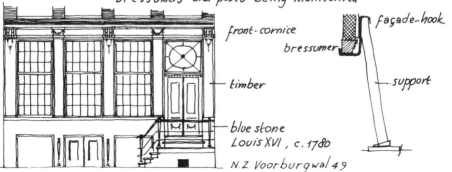

front-cornice
bressumer

façade-hook

timber

support

blue stone
Louis XVI, c.1780

N.Z. Voorburgwal 49

60

the street. This is known as a cornice front. The small loft windows are often set into the frieze of the cornice. Above this runs a partly see-through construction (the attic), usually with a large sculpted showpiece in the middle, often with the coat-of-arms of the owner.

There were also attempts to make the roofs of narrower façades more or less flat, but this created problems. That is why in most cases the centre section has a hoist door with an ornament. It was not until the end of the 18th century, when Classicism was again fashionable, that timber cornices were made straight.

Modernization or restoration bring features from various periods to a façade. Renaissance step gables were rebuilt into bell gables; a classical pilaster gable is sometimes given an attic with a new lower roof behind it. A broken brick façade is often replaced with a timber cornice front, above which the roof ridge protrudes.

In general, alterations like these have led to simplification of the façade to make maintenance easier. And economies of scale and ornamentation went hand-in-hand with the financial state of society.

The lower part of a façade is called a lower front. In the late-Middle Ages these were constructed entirely from timber. The lower front consisted of a number of posts between which door and window openings alternated. Leaded glass filled the windows. The 15th century saw the arrival of brickwork for the section of the façade above the lower front. The brickwork rested

on the front beam or bressumer, which lay across the posts of the lower front. Each storey of a timber façade leant a little forward and that effect was strengthened by allowing the top part of the front beam to protrude and by decorating it with carvings.

The top row of openings was filled with leaded glass. Underneath ran a line of shutters which were used as display shelves for merchandise. The lower half of the shutters folded downwards and the upper half folded upwards as protection against sun and rain. Awnings could not be wider than 1.25 m and had to hang at least 2.25 m above the street. This also applied to signboards. In narrow streets nothing could protrude more than 30 cm. No original awnings remain because they needed a lot of maintenance and proved vulnerable to the increasing traffic.

In the 17th century, the lower fronts were still nearly always of timber. Of course they have been regularly modernized over the centuries, for example with timber glass rods and sash windows, but in many places the timber posts still stand. When entresols were added to the tall entrance halls, the layout of the lower front was also adapted where necessary.

Façades with a lower front were still built in the 18th century, but these have a classical layout, pilaster-type window dams and a cornice above the windows of the main floor. Sometimes the timber lower front was completely replaced with a brick lower front. Even then the front beam was often retained, because the upper façade needed support during modernization.

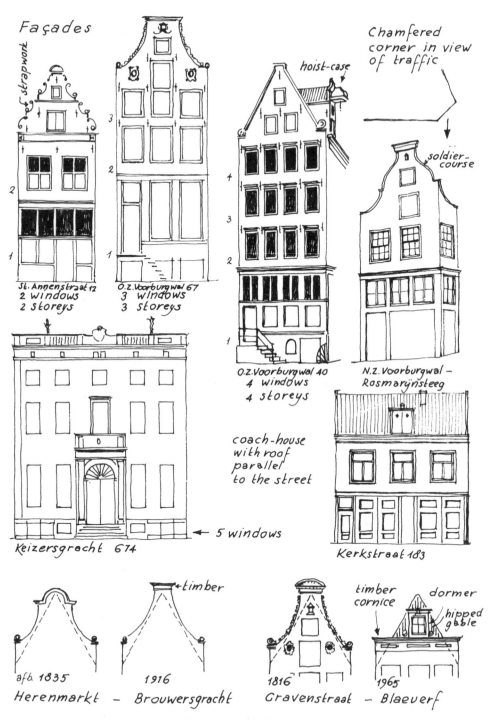

Façades

strapwork

St. Annenstraat 12
2 windows
2 storeys

O.Z. Voorburgwal 67
3 windows
3 storeys

hoist-case

Chamfered
corner in view
of traffic

soldier-
course

O.Z. Voorburgwal 40
4 windows
4 storeys

N.Z. Voorburgwal –
Rosmarijnsteeg

coach-house
with roof
parallel
to the street

← 5 windows

Keizersgracht 674

Kerkstraat 183

←timber

afb. 1835
Herenmarkt

1916
– Brouwersgracht

timber
cornice

dormer

hipped
gable

1816
Gravenstraat

1965
– Blaeuerf

simplifying of gables

62

Old timber lower fronts can, however, cause problems because the foundations subside or the posts rot. The front beam still offers a solution as it can be shored up with supports and façade hooks. This can be seen in many places in the city centre, particularly on vulnerable corner houses with a timber lower front and front beam on two sides.

Herengracht 476   *1666*
Original façade
cross-bar windows - pediment
high-pitched roof - corner-chimneys

After 1730
Modernized façade
sash-windows - attic
lowered roof - high chimneys

Windows and glass

Windows are necessary to let in daylight and fresh air. A window can be filled with a wooden shutter or with glass. If the opening is divided by a vertical and a horizontal post in the middle, it is known as a crossbar window.

In 1550 sandstone crossbar windows were made in the Bank van Lening (pawnshop) between the Nes and the Oudezijds Voorburgwal. The lower sections have vertical iron bars on the inside to keep out burglars.

The window opening can be filled with a wooden frame which gives support to the surrounding brickwork. In the Netherlands window frames are almost always put in place first and the brickwork laid around them. In most other countries, a hole is made in the wall into which a thin window frame is set. This outer frame contains a second frame which holds the glass and which can swing horizontally or vertically or slide up and down.

Crossbar windows were usual until the end of the 17th century. The upper two openings were filled with glass panes of about 10 x 15 cm. They were held in H-shaped lead strips: leaded glass. Horizontal iron rods strengthened the glass panels. Sometimes leaded glass windows were even set into the frames behind shutters.

A carpenter could earn his masters title if he could make a crossbar window under the supervision of the guild council. This is illustrated on a stone tablet along the Egelantiersgracht in the Jordaan.

When the quality of glass improved around 1650, panes could become larger: about 20 x 25 cm. Lead, however, was too soft to support that size and was therefore replaced with wooden rods.

Frames were also made with two openings next to each other: a gemel window. Gables usually offered too little space on either side of the loft shutter to create a normal window. Oval openings were made, surrounded by natural stone ornamentation. This is called an oeil de boeuf.

The enormous church windows were of leaded glass until the 18th century. They were divided by stone posts and horizontal iron bars. In the 17th and 18th centuries these windows sometimes had an iron harnass, and from around 1800 the rusted sections were replaced by wood. Cast iron windows were also used, the first in the Ronde Lutherse Kerk following the fire of 1822.

Around 1685 a new type of frame appeared: a sash window without a cross, with a fixed upper section and a sliding lower section. The first sash windows had five panes along the width in wooden rods. When the quality of glass again improved around 1750 only four panes were necessary. And around 1800 only three or even two. However, just two were expensive because the panes were so large, and these can only be seen in the stately canal houses. When the house at Herengracht 495 was modernized in 1790, it was given windows with two

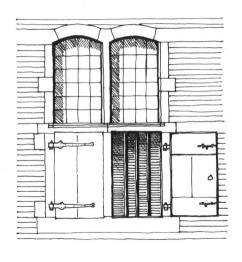

OEIL DE BOEUF
oval loft-window

1550
STONE CROSS-WINDOW
Pawn shop Nes-O.Z. Voorburgwal

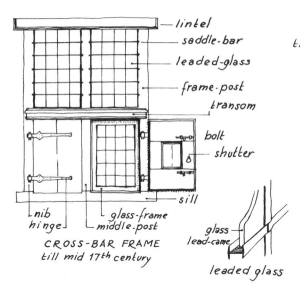

— lintel
— saddle-bar
— leaded-glass
— frame-post
— transom
— bolt
— shutter
— sill

nib
hinge — glass-frame
middle-post

CROSS-BAR FRAME
till mid 17th century

glass
lead-came

leaded glass

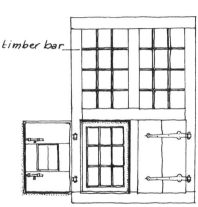

timber bar

CROSS-BAR FRAME
2nd half 17th c.

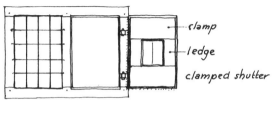

— clamp
— ledge
clamped shutter

GEMEL-FRAME
with leaded-glass

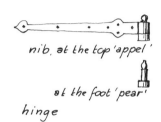

nib, at the top 'appel'

at the foot 'pear'

hinge

panes at the front and three panes at the back. A mocking piece of verse about the then owner said: The owner of this house is the great Six; at the front he looks good but behind he is nix.

At the end of the 18th century French windows came into fashion. These have a thin surround without a frame. They had already been used during the building of the Palace on the Dam in 1650, but it took nearly one and a half centuries before they caught on. Because these windows reach nearly to the floor, they have a little barrier (a French balcony) to stop people falling out of an opened window. The French tax system, introduced in 1811 and in force until 1896, included a tax on doors and windows. No wonder that many windows were bricked up. But in

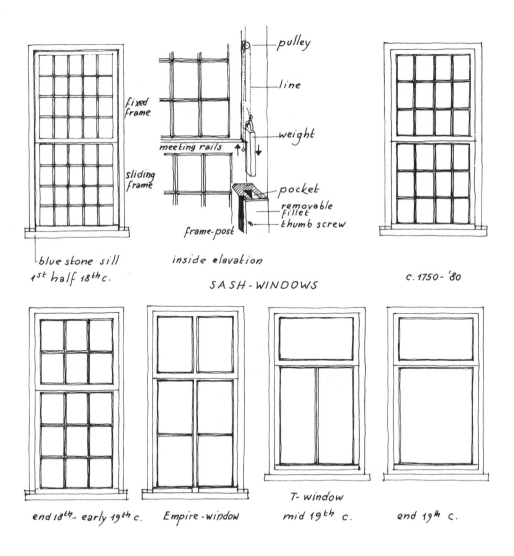

blue stone sill
1st half 18th c.

fixed frame

meeting rails

sliding frame

frame-post

pulley

line

weight

pocket

removable fillet

thumb screw

inside elevation

SASH-WINDOWS

c. 1750- '80

end 18th - early 19th c.

Empire -window

T- window
mid 19th c.

end 19th c.

1833 the tax law was changed to include bricked up windows.

Industrial glass came on the market around 1850. It was cheaper and made it possible to set sash windows with two panes in even the simplest houses. The fixed upper section could then be made from one single pane. In this way the T-window was created.

The Amsterdam School saw a return to smaller panes, but since then the move has been to increasingly large plates of glass, particularly for shop windows. Many frames have been modernized over the centuries and very few crossbar frames remain. Sash windows were given fewer and fewer panes, because people wanted to give their houses a more modern look. During restorations, however, an older style of window is often reinstated.

Glass is not fixed matter, but a cooled liquid which is not crystalized. A mixture of sand, lime and potash or soda is melted at a temperature of around 1100 degrees Centigrade. From the 11th century window glass was made from white hot liquid glass blown into a ball through an iron rod and then flattened to make a disc of several millimetres thick with a diameter of just under a metre. In the 16th century it was also possible to make flat sheets of window glass by shaking out the ball into a cylinder of 40 cm in diameter and 1.20 m in length.

From the 19th century industrial production of glass allowed the hot glass to be drawn upwards between rollers. Once it reached the top, it was cooled and then cut into sheets.

Window glass has to be cut to size. The first method was to use a white hot cutting iron. The upper layer melted and the underneath split. If the split was not exact enough, pieces were broken off. In the 18th century glass was cut with a diamond. These days it is done with a small wheel of hardened steel. The workplaces of glass cutters are often a multicoloured chaos of shards and sheets of glass.

Until around 1550 the pieces cut from glass discs had the shape of a diamond. Later the sheets became ever larger oblongs, but whatever the size or shape, window glass is still known in Dutch as a 'ruit' which also means diamond.

Small amounts of metal oxides in the mixture give colour to glass. Sand often contains some iron which makes the

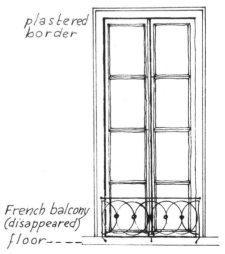

plastered border

French balcony (disappeared)
floor _ _ _ _

French window
French theater – Amstel 56
(Kleine Komedie)
A. v. d. Hart 1786

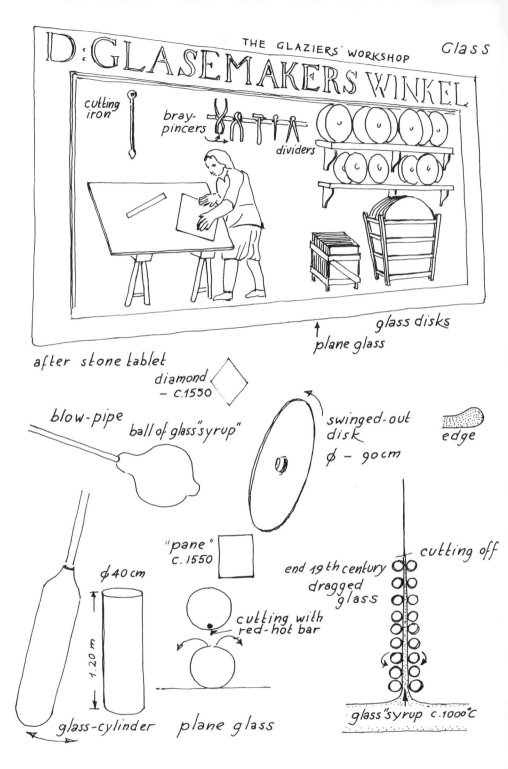

D: GLASEMAKERS WINKEL

cutting iron

bray-pincers

dividers

glass disks

plane glass

after stone tablet

diamond – c.1550

blow-pipe

ball of glass "syrup"

swinged-out disk
ϕ – 90 cm

edge

"pane"
c.1550

ϕ 40 cm

1.20 m

glass-cylinder

plane glass

cutting with red-hot bar

end 19th century
dragged glass

cutting off

glass "syrup" c.1000°C

68

glass green. These panes appear green from the outside, but from the inside the colour is hardly visible. Glass can also discolour. This was the case with a clear sort of glass made in Middle-Germany between 1750 and 1800. When it weathered it turned purple. There are those who still say that the purple colour was the result of a secret process, but the truth is that the glass was of a poor quality. In other words: not a manufacturing secret but a manu-facturing mistake.

Glass can be painted with pictures in dark brown paint. This is then fixed by heating the glass to above 600 degrees Centigrade. This stained glass also has other colours. Coated with a silver compound, it turns deep yellow. The magical effects that can be achieved with stained glass are well illustrated in the Oude Kerk and the Nieuwe Kerk. Mirror glass of about 1 cm thick was cast on a layer of sand. Once it hardened, it was polished on both sides until flat and smooth. The back was given a layer of 'foil', a mixture of tin and mercury, and the air was driven out from between the glass and the foil. It was very unhealthy work and mirror glass panes were never very large. Old mirrors can be recognized from the number of pieces out which they are made.

Stoops

In Amsterdam, the stoop is a paved and sometimes enclosed strip of ground in front of a house. It consists of the steps to the main entrance and a flat area lying a little higher than the street and usually laid with slabs of hard blue stone. The terrain, which belongs to the house, is marked off with hardstone posts, sometimes linked by a chain, or by iron fences. In many places, particularly in narrow streets, the private stoops now belong to the council and are hardly recognizable as belonging to the houses.

The floor of the main storey lies about seven to nine steps above street level. The simplest steps, made from wood or natural stone, run straight up to the door. But in general the steps run parallel to the façade with a landing in front of the door. This allows visitors to walk on and off without immediately finding themselves in traffic. The landing is sometimes at the same level as the interior floor and sometimes one or two steps lower. The fence on the landing often includes a bench.

Narrow houses have a single stoop on one side of the front door; wide houses nearly always have steps on both sides. The simplest steps are oblongs although they usually have rounded edges. In some cases the side is closed in by a decorative sculptured 'harp piece' in natural stone.

The handrail usually rests on cast iron posts (balusters), which could be bought ready-made. Sometimes these are very simple; sometimes they have a special shape reflecting the style in which the stoop was made or modernized. Adriaan Dortsman was the first to put a stoop straight to the façade of the grand canal houses, with an iron fence next to it. This style, based partly on the French example, became quite popular.

The basement door was often under the landing, sometimes next to the steps, with a few steps down. The cellar opening is often covered with a hatch, but sometimes there is a low door giving access to service and storage areas in the basement. Many stoops disappeared in the 19th century when entrances were moved to the basement. Space has always been at a premium in the densely built city centre. The inhabitants of corner houses sometimes solved this by building an extension at cellar level (a cellar shop) for use as storage or workplace. But as early as the 16th century there were regulations preventing unbridled building on the space in front of the houses.

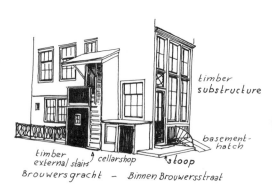

timber
substructure

basement-
hatch

timber
external stairs   cellarshop   stoop

Brouwersgracht — Binnen Brouwersstraat

timber handrail on iron strip

baluster

single-flight perron

Perrons
Stoops

perron bench

basement-entrance

double-flight perron

steps

Regence
Kalkmarkt 7

perron-bench

cast-iron
leaf-baluster

harp-piece
Herengracht 402   1750

Herengracht 452

timber stairs
3rd Weteringdwarsstraat

Keizersgr. 596   Herengr. 460   Herengr. 454   Herengr. 448   Nieuwe
Herengr. 143   Singel 448

Blue stone sideway-poles

71

Ornaments

Many ornaments take their form from nature. In classical architecture much use was made of the acanthus leaf or the Greek bear's-breech, particularly on Corinthian and Composite capitals. In Gothic architecture cabbage and vine leaves were popular.

The Renaissance reflected classical architecture, in particular that of the Romans. The mouldings of the entablature alternate to great effect and a vivid imagination can be seen in the use of stone architraves and cornices – translations of timber sections from ancient Greece – as decoration. There are also candelabra and balusters. As well as the acanthus leaf, there was another favourite motif: the lion mask, which appears as a stone tablet in a frieze. Also from nature came the lobe ornament, often included in the mid-17th century work of the Lutma brothers.

The Romans hung garlands of stone flowers and fruit on their buildings. Dutch classicism also often used these so-called festoons, in stone on façades and painted and gilded indoors. The festoon is often hung on sculpted knobs with sculpted ribbons. Ribbons returned in the ornaments of Louis XVI, but in pleated form.

The Louis styles used the acanthus leaf in countless variations. Shells too were used: stylized and very symmetric in Dutch Renaissance, in bizarre forms in Louis XV or Rococo, amongst other things for garden decoration. Stylized flowers return as rosettes in the Renaissance and in the 19th century even as façade cramps.

At the end of the 18th century much use was made of Greek ornaments like the palmet (a stylized palm leaf) and the Greek fret (meander) which represents the winding course of the river Meander in the Middle East.

All these ornaments were used to great effect in the fanlights above doors. They are usually carved from wood but were sometimes made in richly gilded wrought iron. In the 18th century the owners of the houses often had their initials worked in. This sort of decorative wrought iron is also seen in stoop fences along the canals.

Stone tablets also offered excellent possibilities for ornamentation. They are a permanent reminder of the earlier signboards.

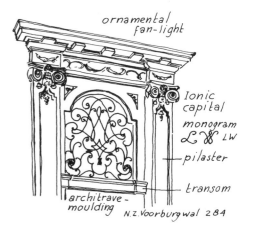

ornamental fan-light

Ionic capital

monogram
LW

pilaster

transom

architrave-moulding

N.Z. Voorburgwal 284

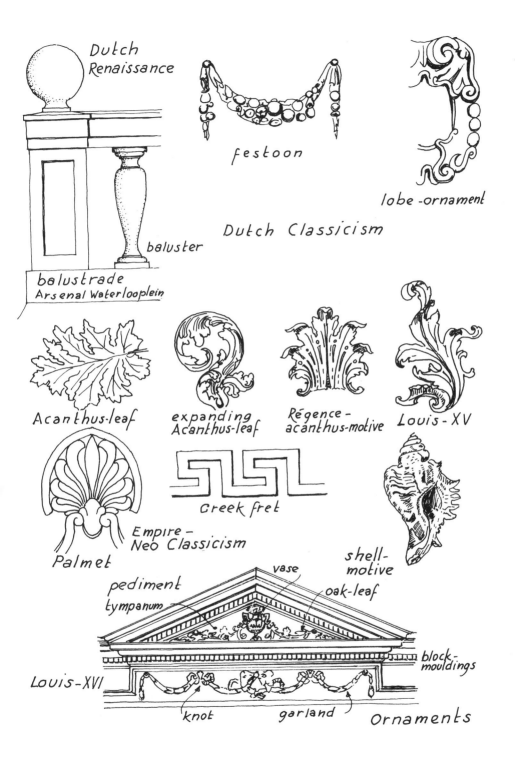

Dutch
Renaissance

festoon

lobe - ornament

Dutch Classicism

baluster

balustrade
Arsenal Waterlooplein

Acanthus-leaf

expanding
Acanthus-leaf

Régence -
acanthus-motive

Louis - XV

Palmet

Greek fret

Empire -
Neo Classicism

shell-
motive

pediment

vase

oak-leaf

tympanum

block-
mouldings

Louis-XVI

knot

garland

Ornaments

Hoist beams

People from out of town are always struck by the fact that every Amsterdam house has a beam with a hook protuding from the façade. These are still used for hoisting goods and moving furniture. Not everyone owns a hoist rope but it is still possible to hire a 'rope and tackle'.

The hoist beam has been part of building regulations for centuries. In earlier times, goods were transferred to barges on the IJ and brought by canal to the merchant's house or to the warehouse. They were hoisted into the house directly from the barge. The 17th century houses usually had narrow stairs, so that household items also had to be hoisted through the windows.

Every house therefore has a hoist beam, which protrudes just under a metre from the façade and is securely fixed to the roof beams. In merchant houses and warehouses a wooden winch was housed in the attic. This had one or two wooden hoist wheels with a series of iron gaffs on the edge. Over these ran an endless rope, which could be reached from all the storage lofts through holes in the floor. A thick rope was wound around the winch, which ran along the hoist beam through the gable and down to the street. Because the façade was built 'in flight', there was space enough on the street to tie the goods to the rope. A man in the loft where the goods were stored could use the endless rope to haul them up. When they reached the appropriate height, he could pull the package through the hoist door.

In a few houses and large warehouses the winch protrudes through the façade and the hoist rope is wound directly onto the axle on the outside. The winch is mounted inside on the axle. The section outside the façade is covered with a large and sometimes decorative winch case. If the façade gores (is built oblique to the house), the hoist beam lies along the length of the house. The hoist wheel then stands parallel to the side walls of the house.

Hoist beams are covered with a small roof of lead or zinc to prevent them from rotting. Around the underside of the beam there is usually also a separate protection for the rope and the hoist hook.

On the smartest houses a hoist beam was an intrusive feature in the façade. In these cases the beam was placed on rollers so that it could be pulled out. Only a hoist door is visible in the façade, behind which sits the hoist beam.

Step gables with a top pilaster also present problems, because there is no room for a hoist beam. Instead these façades have a hoist anchor. The same goes for some simple houses and dormer windows.

From the Amsterdam School there are iron constructions with a hoist hook, which are reminiscent of the old hoist anchors.

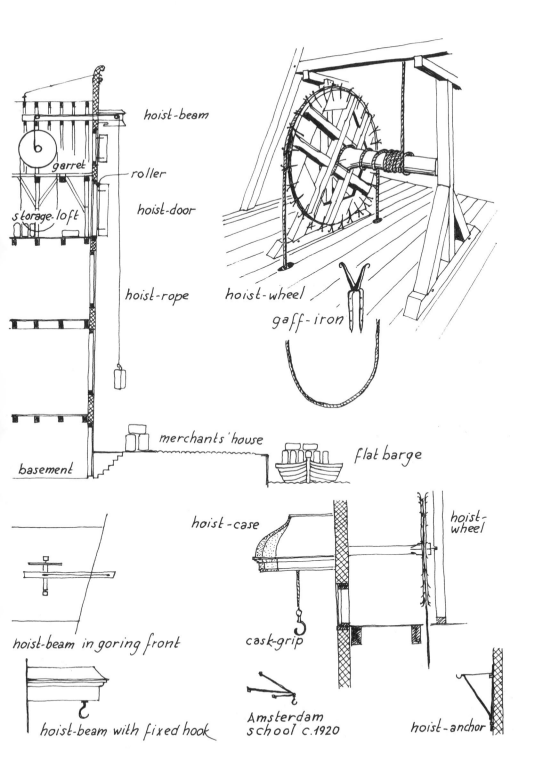

hoist-beam

garret

roller

storage-loft

hoist-door

hoist-rope

hoist-wheel

gaff-iron

basement

merchants' house

flat barge

hoist-case

hoist-wheel

hoist-beam in goring front

cask-grip

hoist-beam with fixed hook

Amsterdam school c.1920

hoist-anchor

75

Warehouses

Large amounts of merchandise, brought by ship to Amsterdam from around the world, were transferred to barges on the IJ. These carried the merchandise to warehouses, which nearly always stood on the water. In those days you could tell what was being stored from the smell on the outside. Some contained cinnamon or stockfish, others barrels of whale oil. Warehouses were much deeper than houses because daylight did not need to reach the centre. In general the storeys were also lower than those in houses, because merchandise was stored by hand and could not be piled too high. In addition, the wooden beams could not bear too much weight. Along the length of large warehouses, under the ordinary beams, ran another beam as extra support. This rested on tie-beam supports. The storeys were reached by a small staircase to one side.

Some façades cover two or three warehouses, each with its own roof. Between them run valley gutters. These warehouses can be recognized by the drainpipe at the height of the valley gutters. In some cases, the water is drained over the loft to a gutter on the side through an open, so-called hidden gutter.

The hoist doors generally stand in a series one above the other. The floor beams are visible between the doors. They often have an iron sheet or trellis as protection for the merchandise during hoisting. Sometimes there is an iron roller, along which the hoist rope has free play during hoisting.

The merchandise often belonged to one of the trading companies, and you can still see warehouses which belonged to the East India Company (VOC), the West India Company (VWC) and the Greenland Company. Many rows of warehouses have individual names from a series: Faith, Hope and Charity, for

Warehouses
Oude Schans

burned down 1949
Korendrager

Grote Zwaan   KleineZwaan
Big Swan   Small Swan

example, were used for storing tobacco. As trading and transport patterns changed, the warehouses lost their original function. Over the years many have been turned into living accommodation. It would obviously be impractical to use the whole depth for just one apartment. A section is therefore often removed from the middle of the building to create a light shaft with two apartments per storey. Renovated warehouses look quite different. Not only are the hoist doors always open, but the openings have been filled with windows. The difference is particularly noticable in the evening. Once rows of warehouses were dark; these days they are brightly lit.

Despite this difference, it is good news from a cultural-historic point of view that the old warehouses are again in use.

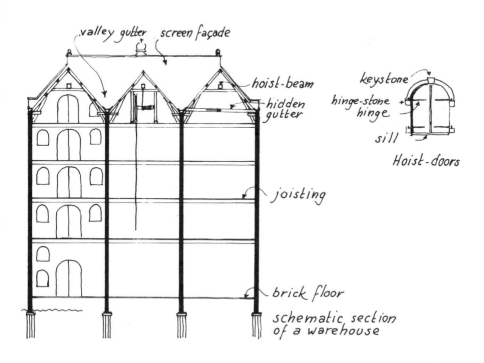

valley gutter   screen façade

hoist-beam
hidden gutter

keystone
hinge-stone
hinge
sill

Hoist-doors

joisting

brick floor

schematic section of a warehouse

Houses

The first houses were built around 1200, with their shortest side on the Amstel. A house was up to 10 metres deep and 3.5 to five metres wide. The walls were of planks or thin woven alder or willow twigs, which grew profusely in the marshlands. The floors were of trodden loam on which lay woven mats. There was an open fire in the living space.

In the countryside around Amsterdam the roofs of the houses were supported by a row of trusses. Outside the truss posts was a low space: a side aisle. The roof of the living space was raised on the sunny side. The closely packed houses along the Amstel dikes let in no light along the side, and the side aisles disappeared. The houses stood about half a metre apart and rain water dripped into a groove between the houses: the eavesdrop.

The oldest houses only had space on the ground floor. The loft could not be used because of soot and smoke. It was only when the chimney was introduced that the loft could be used. From about 1350, two storeys were built, and from then on gradually more. The first brick houses were built in the 14th century. When timber houses were given brick side walls, the eavesdrop disappeared and party walls were built. The beams of both houses lay in one wall but not necessarily at the same height. This also applied to the roof ridges.

No cellars were constructed because of the high water level. There was a space under the ground floor but it was more of a semi-basement. Typical is the floating cellar; a large brick tank within the walls, which more or less floats on the ground water. This kept the water out of the cellar. There were also rain water tanks lined with green and yellow glazed tiles.

A house style arrived in the 15th century with a tall entrance hall, sometimes as much as four metres high. The beams above this extended through to the back façade, but in the back part of the house the floor lay as much as 1.5 metres above street level. This created the mezzanine room. Beneath it was the basement with its floor one metre below street level.

On one side of the high entrance hall there was sometimes a wooden hanging room which could be used for sleeping or working. Often the whole entrance hall had an entresol, which can be seen through the windows of the front façade.

Once houses had more than one storey, stairs were obviously necessary. The earliest were made by placing steps in a spiral around a wooden pole, with a landing on each storey. It was not until the 17th century that straight staircases were made, divided with landings so that the next flight continued in another direction. The graceful architecture of the Louis periods needed an opulent staircase with spacious turns and richly decorated with wood and plaster work.

The floor of the entrance hall and the back part of the house were on the same level in the 17th century, so that the basement stretched the whole depth

Houses

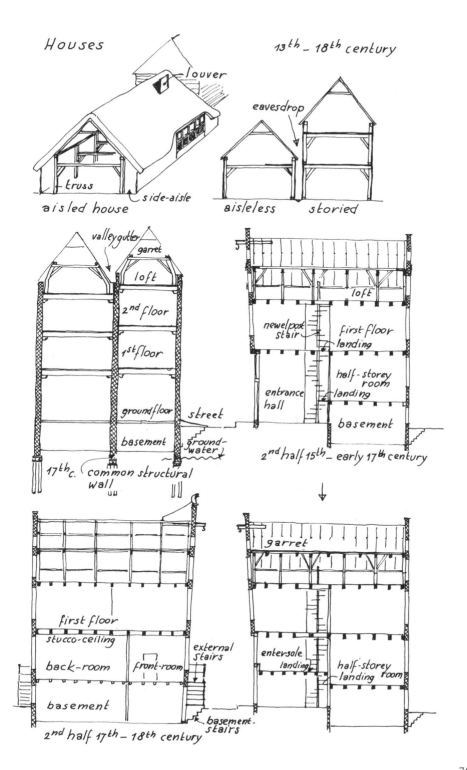

13th – 18th century

louver

eavesdrop

truss

side-aisle

aisled house

aisleless   storied

valleygutter

garret

loft

2nd floor

1st floor

groundfloor

street

basement

groundwater

17th c. common structural wall

loft

newelpost stair

first floor landing

half-storey room landing

entrance hall

basement

2nd half 15th – early 17th century

first floor

stucco-ceiling

back-room   front-room

external stairs

basement

basement stairs

2nd half 17th – 18th century

garret

entersole landing

half-storey room landing

and the floor of the main storey lay one or two metres above street level. The basements of substantial houses contained work and living space for household personnel, such as the kitchen. They had their own entrances on the front, with a few steps down. In less substantial streets the basement contained a workplace or shop, sometimes even living accommodation.

There are two main types of houses in the city centre. On single lots of 5.6 to 8.5 metres wide narrow, deep houses were built. On double lots of 14 to 17 metres wide houses were built, usually wider than they are deep. In 1622 Jacob van Campen designed a double house behind one façade for the Coymans brothers: now Keizersgracht 177. The Trippenhuis on Kloveniersburgwal was designed in 1662 by Justus Vingboons for the Trip brothers, merchants in iron, cannons and tar. In classical style, the front façade has an uneven number of windows along the width. The wall between each house is exactly in the middle and therefore in the middle of the central window. Many merchants used the attic and loft of their canal houses for storing merchandise. You can see this from the sill of the middle window which is a little lower than the others. There is also a loft door with a smaller door above it to the attic.

Not only private houses were built. Institutions built houses to rent as income for their activities. Rented houses for the less well-off were also built, often on speculation. These can sometimes be recognized from a row of identical façades. One house contained more than one home; for example, in the cellar, on the ground floor and upper accommodation which included the loft.

Old and needy citizens, mostly women, were offered free accommodation in almshouses. These were usually built around an inner courtyard or garden (hof). The accommodation often consisted of just one room with a fireplace for heating and cooking and a cupboard bed. Water was fetched from the pump in the courtyard, where the shared clock and privy also stood. Nowadays modernized almshouses are very popular.

There are also large buildings where the old and needy were housed in large dormatories. Some of these old people's homes have been modernized and are still used for the same purpose. One of the best known is Amstelhof, beautifully situated on the Amstel between the Blauwbrug and the Magere brug.

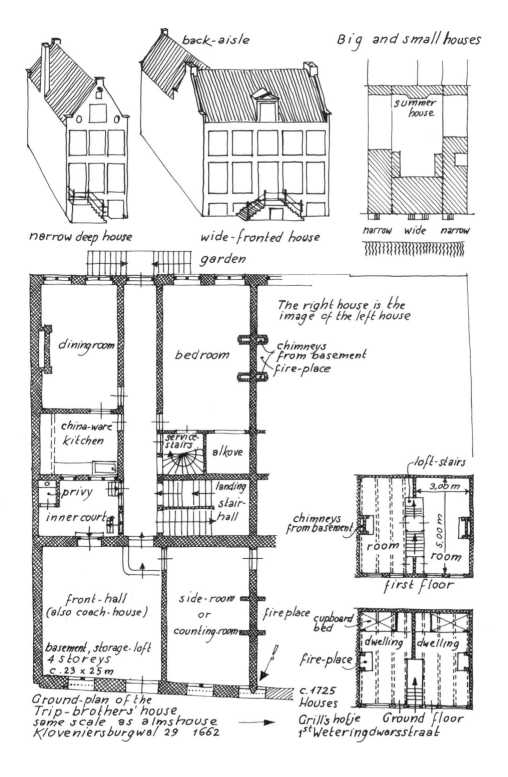

back-aisle

Big and small houses

summer house

narrow deep house

wide-fronted house

narrow   wide   narrow

garden

The right house is the image of the left house

dining room

bedroom

chimneys from basement fire-place

china-ware kitchen

service-stairs

alkove

privy

landing

inner court

stair-hall

loft-stairs

3,00 m

chimneys from basement

5,00 m

room

room

first floor

front-hall (also coach-house)

side-room or counting-room

fireplace

cupboard bed

basement, storage-loft 4 storeys c. 23 x 25 m

fire-place

dwelling   dwelling

Ground-plan of the Trip-brothers' house same scale as almshouse Kloveniersburgwal 29 1662

c. 1725 Houses

Grill's hofje 1st Weteringdwarsstraat

Ground floor

Layout of houses

The first houses consisted of just one room. In the 15th century the space was partitioned by a wooden wall with glass windows, roughly in the middle between the front and back façades. This created an entrance hall for use as work space or entrance porch (hall), and a rear room which could be heated. The mezzanine room soon followed, with the basement beneath it. Usually there was an upper storey for accommodation and the storage of merchandise. A newel post stair stood against the dividing wall, giving access to every storey in the house, from basement to loft.

The floor of the entrance hall was raised in the late-16th century and a separate side room with its own fireplace was created.

The inhabitants of the canal houses often needed more space for their extravagant lifestyle. It was only possible to create two rooms, one behind the other, in corner houses on a side street or alley. In a house with an adjoining plot on each side, no light reached the middle room. A back house was therefore built a few metres behind the main house, linked by a passage. The courtyard ensured light. On the first storey of the main house there were living rooms and bedrooms with above them the storage lofts.

Double houses offered a lot more space and no back house was needed. The staircase was an important feature. There was usually a skylight in the roof above it, allowing daylight to reach the middle of the house. The basement was completely given over to housekeeping and staff accommodation. These canal houses seldom had a storage loft.

Front steps and landing were removed from many houses in the 19th century, and the only entrance was through the basement.

Working class houses had a simpler layout. The workers lived in rented houses with several front doors: an entrance to the basement and two doors on the stoop leading to the lower and upper floors. The industrial revolution of the 19th century did not improve living standards for these people. In working class areas many four storey houses were built. The upper accommodation consisted of one room in either the front or back of the house, with an alcove in both rooms in the partition between them. There was just one toilet per storey. Strange Dutch addresses like 'three up back' date from this period.

Housing associations sprang up in the second half of the 19th century. Their aim was decent accommodation for the workers. Their struggle was rewarded at the beginning of the 20th century when much better blocks of flats were built, partly through the activities of the Amsterdam School architects. However, rooms and windows were still rather small and window sills high. It was only after 1940 that things improved and every home also had a reasonable bathroom.

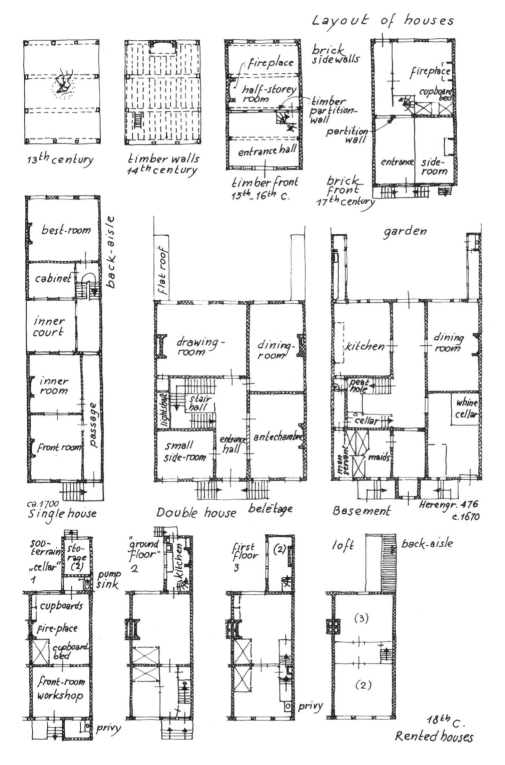

Layout of houses

13th century

timber walls
14th century

fireplace
half-storey room
timber partition-wall
entrance hall
timber front
15th–16th C.

brick sidewalls

fireplace
cupboard bed
partition wall
entrance
side-room
brick front
17th century

best-room
cabinet
inner court
inner room
front room
back-aisle
passage
ca.1700
Single house

flat roof
drawing-room
dining-room
lightshaft
stair hall
small side-room
entrance hall
antechambre
Double house   belétage

garden
kitchen
peat hole
cellar
main servant
maids
dining room
whine cellar
Basement
Herengr. 476
c.1670

sou-terrain "cellar" 1
sto-rage (2)
pump sink
cupboards
fire-place
cupboard bed
front-room workshop
privy

"ground floor" 2
kitchen

first floor 3   (2)
privy

loft   back-aisle
(3)
(2)

18th C.
Rented houses

Fireplaces and chimneys

The oldest fireplace was an open fire in the middle of the room. The smoke spiralled up and out through an opening in the roof. Such houses remained in use on the island of Marken until the 20th century. The danger of fire in Amsterdam brought regulations as early as the 15th century that smoke and sparks must be carried through a brick chimney. No timber could be used, but the occasional beam did protrude into the flue, which sometimes led to a vigorous fire in the chimney! One or two small beams (laths) were allowed in a chimney for hanging meats to smoke.

The fireplace was built against a wall. The chimney breast, which ran right up to the loft, caught the smoke. Sometimes the chimney breast was surrounded by a wooden mantelpiece. The hearth was of brick or had a cast iron grate. The back wall of the hearth was protected by special fireproof bricks and later by a decorative cast iron plate. Fires were not allowed to burn at night. The last embers went into a covered pot or a brick-lined hole next to the fireplace.

Old chimneys were roomy. Excess smoke from wood and peat was dispersed by the up draught and sparks had to be extinguished before they entered the flue. Chimney sweeping was done by boys, mainly the sons of Italian chimney sweeps, who scrambled from top to bottom and emerged covered in soot. This is how the story of Black Peter (assistant to Saint Nicholas) and the parcels from the chimney originated.

The chimney was an important feature in finishing off the roof of a classical building. Because it did not run straight up from the fireplace, supports had to be constructed to carry it through the roof. Large chimney openings were given a cover – often with a tall cap and sometimes even a weathervane – to keep out as much rain and snow as possible.

Fireplaces were smaller in the 18th century, because different fuel was used which gave more smoke. This requires a stronger up draught. The chimney breast was lowered and the opening of the flue made smaller. These so-called English fireplaces stand on marble hearths lined with cast iron plates. The cast iron stove arrived in the 19th century and open fires were no longer used.

A chimney frequently drew badly, for example because a nearby tall building caused the wind to swirl over the roof. In this case, a wooden construction with two or more openings was added. Some of these were so bizarre that they did nothing for the look of the city. A rotating cap could be added, which moved in the wind. This is known as a chimney jester or turn cap.

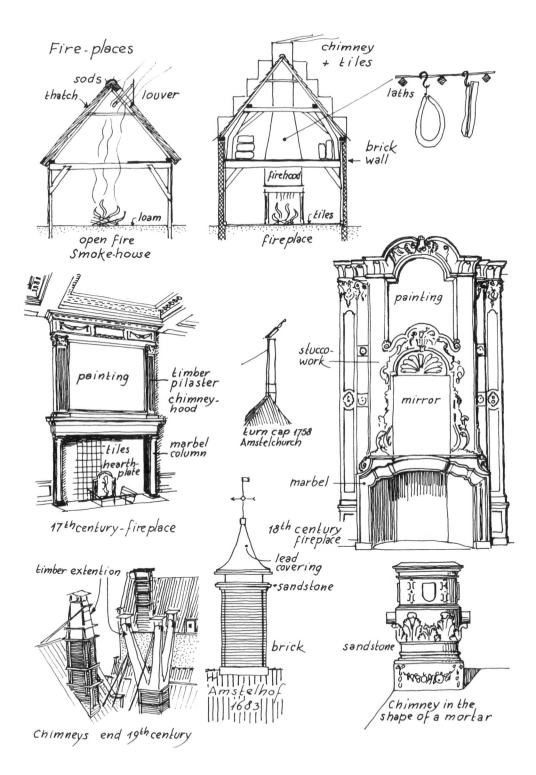

Fire-places

sods
thatch   louver
open fire
Smoke-house
loam

chimney + tiles
laths
brick wall
firehood
fireplace
tiles

painting
timber pilaster
chimney-hood
tiles
hearth-plate
marbel column
17th century - fireplace

turn cap 1758
Amstelchurch

painting
stucco-work
mirror
marbel
18th century fireplace

timber extention
Chimneys end 19th century

lead covering
sandstone
brick
Amstelhof 1683

sandstone
Chimney in the shape of a mortar

Interiors

It was not until the mid-17th century that a visual cohesion was created between ceiling, walls, floor and furnishing. Spacial totality dates from the 18th century. Slowly the visible structure of the building disappeared behind a veneer. Originally the brick walls were plastered white, over which wall coverings were sometimes hung. In the 17th and 18th centuries, important rooms were hung with gold leather: strips of painted leather were stitched together and embossed with a variety of motifs. Large parts of the surface were covered in a layer of silver leaf and varnished, which gave it a gold colour. The fireplace was an important feature in the 17th century interior. Around 1700 large paintings on canvas were stretched into moulded frames, at first broken up into small individual frames and later also as a continuous picture over doors and in corners of the room.

Stucco became an important feature in the 18th century. Decoration in the reigning style softened the severity of the straight walls. Gilding and paint-work emphasized the luxurious effect. Fretwork, stucco work, mirrors, representations in colour or grisaille were introduced over doors and on mantelpieces.

Things sobered down in the 19th century. There were fewer paintings and walls coverings were sometimes made in expensive material like damast. Wall-paper made its entrance at the end of the 18th century. At first it was printed with wooden blocks or hand-painted. In the course of the 19th century more and more industrially produced wall-paper was used in ordinary houses, which until then had usually had simple whitened walls.

In modest houses and less important parts of large houses dividing walls were usually just a wooden partition, often painted in simple colours. Until the 17th century, the ceiling consisted of cross-beams and joists, which were often painted. Later the joists were sometimes panelled, although the cross-beams remained visible. These ceilings were painted with tendrils and imitation fretwork, mainly gilded. When the joists disappeared, the ceiling under the beams was painted. It was not until the end of the 17th century that orna-mental stucco ceilings appeared. In the centre there was a painting of the sky with clouds and floating figures.

The floors in the basements were generally of stone and on upper storeys almost always wood, sometimes painted. Painted canvas was also used. Halls and passages had natural stone tiles or large slabs laid on shells over the wooden floor. White veined marble was sometimes laid symmetrically, like the pages of an open book. This is even called à livre ouvert.

The hallway of a narrow house had doors giving access to the rooms along just one side. Sometimes fake doors were made for the opposite wall to suggest that the house had rooms on both sides. Sometimes doors were even made to appear larger than they actually were. In the 18th century, walls were decorated with stucco work and plaster statues.

In the same period, staircases became a status symbol with abundantly carved bannisters, stucco decorations and a skylight above them.

The courtyard was visually joined to the interior by the use of statues.

Interiors

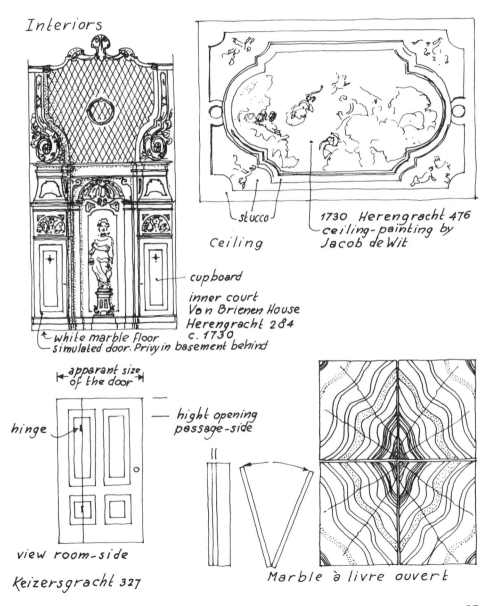

stucco

Ceiling

1730 Herengracht 476
ceiling-painting by
Jacob de Wit

cupboard

inner court
Von Brienen House
Herengracht 284
c. 1730

white marble floor
simulated door. Privy in basement behind

apparent size
of the door

hinge

hight opening
passage-side

view room-side

Keizersgracht 327

Marble à livre ouvert

87

Gardens and garden houses

In the densely built centre of Amsterdam along the canals virtually the only space for gardens is behind the houses built for merchants and governors. During the city expansion of the 17th century regulations (keuren) were brought in for a number of building plots along the new canals to restrain construction within them. These regulations are still in force and these blocks of houses are known as 'keur' blocks.

From the slightly higher placed room at the back of the house there is a wonderful view of the garden, laid out to the taste of the time and the financial position of the owner. Usually there was a well-made, geometric ornamental garden, where straight hedges and paths bordered flower beds, statues and ponds. A fountain, a bird-house and a sundial completed the picture.

The Louis XV or Rococo style made great use of shells for garden ornamentation, on fountains or in shell grottos, those romantic semi-dark fake works of plaster. Sometimes there was room for a kitchen garden and fruit trees. There was a small bleaching field for the washing.

In the 19th century the rectangular layout gave way to a wilder, more natural style with large old trees as a popular feature.

At the bottom of the garden there was usually a summerhouse where family and visitors could relax. It was just one storey high, often had a flat roof and was combined with the summer kitchen. These summerhouses often had a monumental character that fitted in with the style of the garden. There were also smaller, partly open arbours. Sometimes the building at the bottom of the garden had a more permanent character with an upper storey. Downstairs was usually a summer room just like a summerhouse. The upper floor, with a separate entrance, was used as an office, study or library. In winter these rooms could be heated. The blocks of houses between two canals met at the bottom of their gardens, with garden houses back to back. Where a street runs between two canals, coachhouses were built with stabling and room for the family coach. Upstairs was living space for the staff. In particularly large coachhouses the attics could also be used for storage. The richly ornamented back façade serves as a background to the garden. A summerhouse was also often included. With few canal houses still in use as homes, it is rare to find gardens which are layed out in the original manner and used for entertainment. The trees have grown into centuries old giants which give a lot of shadow. But the simple and rich garden houses still stand. Even today, the hidden gardens and courtyards form an oasis of peace in the busy city.

Summer- and coach-houses

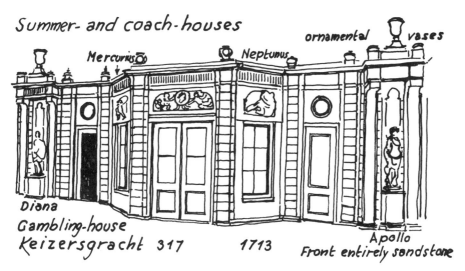

ornamental vases

Mercurius

Neptunus

Diana

Apollo

Gambling-house
Keizersgracht 317   1713   Front entirely sandstone

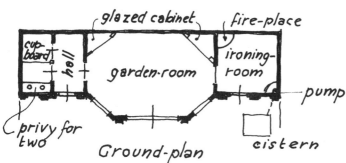

glazed cabinet

fire-place

cup-board

hall

garden-room

ironing-room

pump

privy for two

cistern

Ground-plan

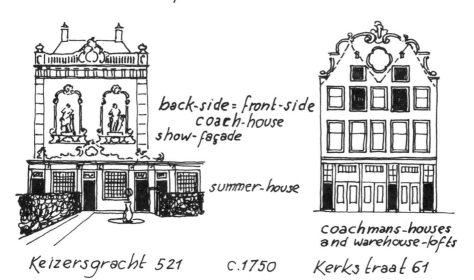

back-side = front-side
coach-house
show-façade

summer-house

coachmans-houses
and warehouse-lofts

Keizersgracht 521   c.1750   Kerkstraat 61

Interior decoration

There was a time when building materials were chosen on the basis of suitability and price and not, like now, also for the effects of colour and texture. Architecture was a game of coloured areas between sharp lines. Brick, wood and lead were usually painted, often in a very different colour to the material itself. The paint also formed a protection against the weather and rotting.

Façades were painted to achieve a uniform colour. In the 16th and 17th centuries the paint was mainly red to match the Leiden bricks, but in the 18th century, when improved quality brought a darker brick, the paint was brown. Bentheim sandstone is porous and turns black. To retain the original light ochre colour and to ensure a watertight surface, the stone was always painted in the 'Bentheim' colour. Even timber sections were sometimes painted to look like natural stone. Doors and window frames were generally of oak. 'The unpretentious and multi-coloured wood was often painted in one colour', wrote a painter around 1800. Frames were painted white with oil paint in the 17th century; doors and shutters red, green, yellow ochre or brown. After 1700 doors were olive green and the panels of shutters orange-red, white or blue-green. Sash windows, becoming popular at that time, were painted white and after 1770 also green.

Frames were given the colour of grey sandstone. Around 1880 doors and shutters were glossy dark brown, but within a few years this was already old fashioned. That was when the green colour arrived which still dominates the look of the city, although over the years many different shades have appeared. The genuine 'canal green' was created around 1830 from a mixture of Berlin blue (a poisonous iron-cyanide binding element), yellow ochre and Bremen green (copper oxide). Legend has it that the doors were painted green because there was a tax on oak in Louis Napoleon's time. The origin of this tale can probably be found in the very short-lived fashion for brown painted doors. Between 1811 and 1896 there was a tax on the number of outer doors.

Wood was often painted to look like marble. This was obviously cheaper than the real thing. Only touch reveals the secret. Wood was often also painted to look like a more expensive variety.

In every season and all weathers Amsterdam is attired in different colours. On a bright summer's day the dark green trees are set off by the green of doors and windows and the red and purple of brick. On a misty autumn morning the city is covered by a grey veil. In freezing weather everything is sharply defined and blue-grey in colour. But Amsterdam is at her loveliest in the spring, when the budding trees give a green haze along the façades and the blue sky is mirrored in the windows of the canal houses.

Glossary

* see separate entry

Architrave beam resting on upper part of column. Also often used independently as moulded door frame.

attic storey immediately under roof; storey above façade cornice which often blocks view of roof. Also loft.

baluster short pear-shaped pillar to support handrail.

balustrade row of balusters with coping for parapet.

beading narrow cylindrical moulding.

beam weight-bearing horizonal part of construction, usually a long rectangular piece of timber.

binder main beam carrying *joists.

breast protruding part of *chimney to catch smoke, often fitted with *mantelpiece.

bridge gap opening in centre of bridge for passage of ships; covered with two movable sections.

bulwark jutting part of defensive fortification.

candelabrum tall candlestick-shaped decorative feature.

cantilever overhanging or projecting part of wall.

casement timber frame within *window frame to carry glass, and which can swing or slide.

cellar shop extension of basement onto part of stoop.

channel rafter internal corner between two intersecting roof areas.

chimney structure by which smoke is carried off.

claw piece carved feature on both sides of upright part of top gable.

closer one-quarter brick.

collar stone carved stone on which post or vaulting rests.

colossal order pillars in particular order over more than one storey.

corbel stone or timber projection from wall supporting posts.

cornice horizontal moulded projection crowning building.

cross-beam foundation framework of beams into gaps of which piles are driven to form *foundation.

cross frame timber or stone window frame divided into four parts.

cupboard bed bed closed off from room in specially built cupboard.

curved brace strengthening piece between post and beam in timber constructions, generally curved.

Dutch arch wide wedge-shaped brick span for a window opening, *stretch.

entablature *architrave, *frieze and *cornice of column.

entresol low storey between first and ground floors; *hanging room.

fanlight *light above a door.

festoon hanging chain of flowers, leaves and fruits carved in stone.

fireplace grate or hearth in room.

flagstone fired floor tile.

foot measurement of length. An Amsterdam foot is 28.3 cm.

foundation underground support of building.

foundation cross-beam linking beam over the heads of foundation piles.

foundation pile vertically sunk length of heavy timber, sometimes concrete, for support of building.

frieze flat part of *entablature between *cornice and *architrave.

front beam beam across lower front that carries brick upper façade.

garret room on top floor.

gored not squared to the axle of a building.

half pillar semi-circular pillar against façade.

hanging room wooden chamber hung from ceiling beams and walls, generally in part of entrance hall; *entresol.

harp piece slab of stone with arched top, which closes off the side of a flight of *stoop steps.

head short side of brick.

hinge movable joint on which door or *shutter swings.

hip rafter intersecting line of two roof areas, meeting under an external corner.

hipped gable slanted section above upper part of roof end.

hoist beam protruding beam at top of façade with which to hoist goods.

hoist door door in façade through which goods can be hoisted in.

hoist wheel wheel fitted to wooden *winch around which hoist rope is wound.

joist one of row of parallel timbers to carry floor.

landing platform at top of stairs or to break up flights of steps.

lift-lock *lock for bringing ships from one water level to another.

light part of window through which light falls; *fanlight.

lock section of river or canal confined between sluice gates.

lock post vertical post of *sluice door.

mantelpiece structure above and around *fireplace.

mezzanine low storey between two others, particularly ground and first floors but also under roof.

monk circular pillar on stone dam.

oeil de boeuf oval window, generally with carved outer frame.

parapet low wall at edge of roof, balcony, bridge; mound along front of trench.

pediment triangular or arched feature crowning gable, *window or entrance in classical style.

pilaster rectangular *pillar projecting from wall, with capital of classical pillar style.

pillar slim upright structure supporting arch or other architectural weight.

pinnacle slim Gothic feature in form of tower.

portico yoke of two posts linked by beam on which the balance of a leaf bridge rests.

privy simple toilet without flush.

pulse iron tube with lid on lower end which closes as pulse is pulled up; used in reparation of *foundations.

purlin horizontal beam running along length of roof.

rib thin timber beam.

ridge line of junction of two roof surfaces.

ridge tile tile used for *ridge of roof.

rule small horizontal beam between two timber posts.

sash window frame holding *window glass made to slide up and down.

shavings thin slices of oak used as lining between *joists and floor covering.

shutter movable wooden screen for closing off *window opening.

sluice contrivance for controlling flow or volume of water.

soldier course series of bricks laid on their sides.

sole plate elongated flat piece of timber for supporting end of beam.

stone tablet small slab of natural stone in façade with inscription or representation.

stoop paved and sometimes enclosed area in front of house, usually with steps to main entrance.

stoop bench seat on landing of *stoop.

stoop post blue stone post marking extent of *stoop.

storey each horizontally divided section of building.

stretch 1) *Dutch arch; 2) length of brick.

stucco plaster for covering ceilings and walls.

three quarter brick measuring three quarters of usual length.

thumb measure of length; about 2 cm.

top pilaster upper small column of step gable.

transom horizontal beam between door and *fanlight.

truss support structure of *posts, *beam and *curved brace.

tympanum vertical recess, usually triangular, on *pediment.

vault arched structure serving as roof.

volute spiral scroll as ornament of Ionic capital.

wainscot wooden panelling on wall of room.

winch revolving horizontal axle, used for hoisting.

window frame wooden outer frame in which *shutters and *casement are fitted.

Explanation of street names

*see separate entry

Begijnhof pious women who do not wish to enter a convent have lived here as a community since 1346.

Bickerseiland island of reclaimed land in the IJ where Jan Bicker, descendant of a ruling family, had his shipyards.

Bierkade part of the *Oudezijds Voorburgwal south of the Oude Kerk (Old Church), where imported beer was unloaded.

Binnenkant literally 'inside' or inner side of the Waalseiland, reclaimed from the sea in 1646. *Oude Waal, *Buitenkant.

Blaeu-erf, Blaeu-straatje alleyways around *Gravenstraat behind the Nieuwe Kerk (New Church). The son of the famous cartographer Blaeu had his printing works here.

Brouwersgracht a brouwer is a brewer and there were several breweries along this canal.

Buitenkant the 'outside' or outer IJ side of Waalseiland between what are now the Scheepvaarthuis (Maritime House) and the *Melkmarkt (Milk Market). Now part of the *Prins Hendrikkade. *Binnenkant, *Oude Waal.

Damrak straight stretch (rak) of the Amstel, outside the dam.

Eggertstraat runs from the Dam, behind the Nieuwe Kerk to the *Gravenstraat. Willem Eggert gave the ground for the building of the church at the end of the 14th century.

Gasthuismolensteeg between Singel and Herengracht at Paleisstraat. Along the city wall at the Singel stood the mill (molen) of the Hospital (Gasthuis).

Geldersekade the city wall was built here when the city was seriously threatened by troops from Gelderland.

Gravenstraat runs behind the Nieuwe Kerk over terrain which formed the Earl of Holland's garden in the 14th century.

Groenburgwal many weavers were situated along this canal, making green (groen) cloth. *Raamgracht.

Haarlemmer Houttuinen location of timber stores (houttuinen) outside the Haarlemmerdijk.

Heiligeweg only remaining section of road taken by pilgrims between the village of Sloten, along the *Over-toomse Vaart to the Heilige Stede (Holy Place). *Kapelsteeg.

Kalverstraat a calves (kalveren) market was held on the old Amsteldijk between the Dam and Spui.

Kapelsteeg, Wijde-Enge between these alleyways between the *Kalverstraat and *Rokin stood the Heilige Stede (Holy Place). This chapel was built on the site of the house where in 1345 the Holy Miracle took place. A column was erected on Rokin in 1988 to commemorate the chapel, which was demolished in 1912.

Kloveniersburgwal the gunners (kolveniers) practised where the canal at the wall tower Silent Utrecht becomes the Nieuwe Doelenstraat.

Kromboomsloot winding ditch in the Lastage where timber for shipbuilding lay in the water before being sawn.

Melkmarkt milk market where the farmers from Waterland (district north of Amsterdam) unloaded their milk.

Molsteeg the dredgers (baggermolen) for keeping the canals at a good depth were stored here, near the *Nieuwezijds Voorburgwal.

Muntplein the building that replaced the Regulierspoort (gate) in 1619 was used for minting coins from 1672 for over a year. Munt is mint in Dutch. Around 1900 the square was given the name Sophiaplein, after King Willem III's first wife, but the local tradition of calling it Munt proved stronger.

Nes piece of land outside the dike, in this case between the Amsteldijk and the river.

Nieuwebrugsteeg continuation of the Nieuwe Brug (New Bridge), built in the 14th century at the IJ over *Damrak.

Nieuwezijds Voorburgwal first city wall along the Boerenwetering on the Nieuwe Zijde (New Side); after a second outer wall was built Voorburgwal was added.

Nieuwezijdskolk originally a sluice for draining the water from the *Nieuwezijds Burgwal on *Damrak.

Niezel, Lange and Korte corruption of liesdel (reedbed), pool in which irises grow.

Oude Schans the Lastage, which lay outside the city wall, was protected on its eastern side by an earthen wall.

Oude Turfmarkt this part of *Rokin was a peat (turf) market around 1600. It was given back its old name in 1947 but retained the house numbers of Rokin.

Oude Waal quay along an inlet of the IJ, the Oude(zijds) Waal. The curved stretch is called Kromme (crooked) Waal.

Oudebrugsteeg runs to the *Warmoesstraat along the former oldest brigde over *Damrak.

Oudezijds Achterburgwal second city wall on the Oude Zijde (Old Side).

Oudezijds Voorburgwal first city wall on the Oude Zijde.

Oudezijdskolk sluice for draining the water of the Oudezijds Burgwal into the IJ.

Overtoom originally Overtoomse Vaart (waterway), it led to the point where a dam separated the Amsterdam city water from the water level of Rijnland. Small ships were helped over the dam by the 'overtoom': a hand operated slipway.

Prins Hendrikkade the quay along the IJ once bore various names, from east to west *Buitenkant, Kamperhoofd, Oude Teertuinen, Texelsekaai and Haringpakkerij. Around 1880 the whole length was named after King Willem II's youngest son. His bust stands in the garden opposite Central Station.

Raamgracht area outside the city wall where dyed sheets were dried on wooden frames (a frame is a raam).

Realeneiland island in the IJ reclaimed in 1615 and owned by alderman Jacob Reaal.

Rechtboomsloot *Kromboomsloot, recht means straight.

Reguliersbreestraat and Reguliersgracht outside the city walls in the vicinity of the present day Rembrandtplein stood the monastry of the Regulier monks towards which ran a broad street and a canal.

Rokin the straight stretch or rak of the Amstel inside the Dam was known as Rak-in, now Rokin.

Rusland marshland on which grew

reeds of the Juncus family. In Dutch this reed is called a rus.

Singel canal on the western side of the 15th century city wall.

Singelgracht outer canal around the 17th century city wall, along which the Nassaukade, Stadhouderskade and Mauritskade now run.

Sint-Anthoniesbreestraat on the old sea dike outside the city walls stood the Sint-Anthonie Hospital where lepers were nursed.

Sint-Olofspoort and Sint-Olofssteeg the first city gate on the IJ side took its name from the nearby Sint-Olofs chapel, consecrated to the patron saint of Norwegian sailors. The chapel was joined to the neighbouring Heilig Graf chapel to form the Oudezijds chapel.

Spui sluice through which excess water from the Boerenwetering was drained into the Amstel.

Spuistraat formerly Nieuwezijds Achterburgwal.

Staalstraat samples (stalen) of cloth were displayed and traded in the Saai Hall near the *Groenburgwal.

Warmoesstraat vegetable gardens (moes-tuin in Dutch) were located along this Amstel dike.

Weteringschans part of the city wall at the Boerenwetering. The watercourse still forms the water between the Hobbemakade and the Ruysdaelkade.

Zandhoek according to a 1634 regulation, sand barges could only unload along this quay on the IJ side of the *Realeneiland.

Zeedijk dike along the IJ on the Zuiderzee side.